PONDERING THE PAVEMENT

*Sharing Thoughts
Along My Walk*

by
C. A. Filius
America's Extra Large Medium

What Blog Readers Have Been Saying…

"I Love How You Spread The Love To All Of Us All The Time. It takes courage to speak truth and love to the universe. Love surrounds you and you share it. I am grateful to read your words. Thank you."

> "I absolutely LOVE this story! It definitely leaves me wanting to hear MORE!!!"

"Thank you, Charles, for another moving and thought-provoking piece, written from the heart."

> "You are a blessing to our universe! Thank you for sharing your life!"

"This was just beautiful and brought tears!"

> "You made me laugh out loud. Hysterical!!!!!"

"Such an important, beautiful message born out of such tragedy! Thanks for this, Charles!"

> "That's a great story Charles. I love how insistent Gabriel was to get through to you. I can't imagine you ever getting bored by what you do… or spirit ever letting you be bored!"

"Thank you, Charles. We can't be reminded enough of what truly counts in life."

What Blog Readers Have Been Saying…

"I've been thinking about you lots lately so not surprised to read this wonderful story, reminding me of your amazing sense of humor and great connections with the other side."

> "I so enjoyed reading your story of connections and your doubting them… to encourage me to keep believing the connections I get with my loved ones."

"Thank you so much for allowing me to read of your experiences. It resets my heart to read your words… and reminds me how blessed I have been to have had powerful readings by you that connected me to my loved ones… time I will always treasure…"

> "What a loving tribute. I laughed and I cried. What a special bond you both had, the bond of humor, the bond of getting each other's humor with total understanding and enjoyment. It's so great that you had eighteen years of each other. More would have been better, but 18 is so much better than none. Thank you for sharing this wonderful peek into the relationship you had with your birthmom. It is a treasure."

"Reading this I laughed and I cried. The laughter won."

Copyright © 2016 Charles A. Filius

ISBN 13: 978-0-692-79990-1
ISBN 10: 0-692-79990-7

All Rights Reserved. No part of this book may be reproduced, stored in a retrieval system, or transmitted in any form, by any means, including mechanical, electric, photocopying, recording or otherwise, without the prior written permission of the publisher and author.

Inquiries: P O Box 14881 • Long Beach, CA 90853

Printed in the United State of America

Acknowledgements

Mona Masonis-Boyer, Kevin Coburn, Rebeka Lopez,
Shawn Rietsch, April Torres, Dyan Yamaguchi,
John Culbertson, James Powell,
Suzie Estridge, Craig Massey, Kelsey Stirling,
Carol Franko, Stuart Grady, Kat Koszewski, Danielle Potts,
Marianne & Larry Russo,
Darlene & Gregg Spaete,
Todd & Candace Livingston, Robert & Shannon Tinnell,
Woody & Eleanor Rowe,
Markis Newman & Jay Murphy,
Carletta Gould, Audrie Graham, Fred Kitchen,
Maxine Loudermilk, Geri Wilisch
and
Shannon Marie O'Connell

In Loving Memory of

**Ruth R. Powell
&
Everett L. "Kitch" Kitchen**

My Aunt & My Dad

♥

No Greater Love Given
No Greater Laughter Shared

♥

I am Truly Grateful to Both for Both

"One never knows, do one?"

Fats Waller

INTRODUCTION BY JOHN CULBERTSON

My name is John Culbertson. At the time of writing this foreword I've been involved in the New Age, Metaphysical, and Psychic field for nearly 20 years. I've authored three books, have taught a great many classes, and have done private sessions for thousands of people from around the world. This isn't about me though. No, it's about Charles Filius and the endearing masterpiece of insights that you now hold in your hands.

I consider Charles to be not only a colleague of mine, but also one of my dearest friends. I first met Charles when we were studying psychic development in separate classes under the world renowned psychic channel and teacher Sandy Anastasi. Charles and I were then joined together in a class dedicated to not only helping to harness psychic ability, but to help us learn how to teach these skills to others as well.

I found him funny, witty, and highly intelligent. I knew from the moment I first met him that he was going to be a very talented psychic medium. I also knew from the moment that I first met him that he was going to help a whole lot of people. What I didn't know at the time was how great he was at writing, too. It would be several years before that would become apparent to me as he tends to keep his skills close to the vest.

As I read his first book, *On a Wing and a Prayer*, I found myself smiling. I was smiling because of the skill at which Charles crafted every word. I was smiling because he was able to take his own spiritual journey and effortlessly, with humor, bring other people into it. Well, he's managed to do that once again.

The book you now hold is a collection of writings that Charles has done over the years. They come from his personal blog. Each piece, or blog post, carries with it the same craftsmanship that was found within his first two books – *On a Wing and a Prayer* and *Dailies*. You should certainly read both of those, but even if you haven't this current book is a not to be missed attraction.

It seems blogging has become a favorite pastime of many in our world. Why wouldn't it be? After all, it's an avenue of expression that is totally in tune with where our world is heading and also where it has come from. In our digital age, having a blog becomes an extension of the person who writes it. It's like a secret diary of personal thoughts, insights, experiences, and revelations. The difference is that a blog, unlike a diary, is put out there for the world to see.

It takes either a very courageous person or a person who simply doesn't care about the opinions of others to do blogging. Charles is absolutely courageous. In his blogging Charles opens up on a very deep and often times very profound level. He opens up more in his blogging then he sometimes does when you're sitting there with him in person. Sure, the humor is many times found in both cases, but with blogging you get beyond the humor to those things which are truly deep and important.

In this book you will need to be prepared to read about the deeply personal. You'll also read about the profound messages his spiritual guides share with not just him, but with others and the world as a whole. There's a good chance that you'll laugh and, given exactly what you're reading and the mood you find yourself in, you may even cry. You will gain insights not just from what his guides share, but also from being a part of the life of Charles himself. You'll get to share in the inner thoughts of a man that has a big heart, an expansive mind, and an open spirit.

This book is something which I personally believe everyone should truly treasure and be grateful for. By allowing you into his life and his world, you'll get to take Charles's experiences and make them your own. You'll get to take his insights and even make them your own, too. From his family and experiences with synchronicity to his travels and the people he encounters, each and every moment will make you think and ponder and create a sense within yourself that you're glad you're having the opportunity to live through Charles.

I agreed to write this foreword because I not only believe in Charles and his abilities, but also because I know that what Charles puts out there in his writing is guided by spirit of the highest level. There are so few in this field who have the capacity to be as connected to spirit as Charles is – and the thing is, it's not just what they tell him and he pens, but it's the life he lives and the experiences he has on a day-by-day basis that reminds him... indeed all of us... that none of us are ever alone in this journey through life. If we can take solace in anything, it's that each and every one of us as human beings deal with, at some point or another, pain, frustration, and hardships in life. It is, after all, part of the human experience. When we are given the opportunity to see how one person manages to successfully deal with life, live life, and experience life – if we allow ourselves to partake in that, we stand the chance of coming away from it with more understanding and a new outlook on the journey that we all must go through.

As I said at the beginning, this is an endearing master piece. The insights are now yours to take, explore, and absorb. I know they've helped to guide and enlighten me – to help me be a better person, and I've no doubt if given the chance that they'll do the same for you too.

Please enjoy your own Pondering the Pavement.

Rev. John W. Culbertson
Independent Metaphysical Minister • Speaker • Writer
http://www.mysticjohnculbertson.com
Saint Joseph, MO – 10/2016

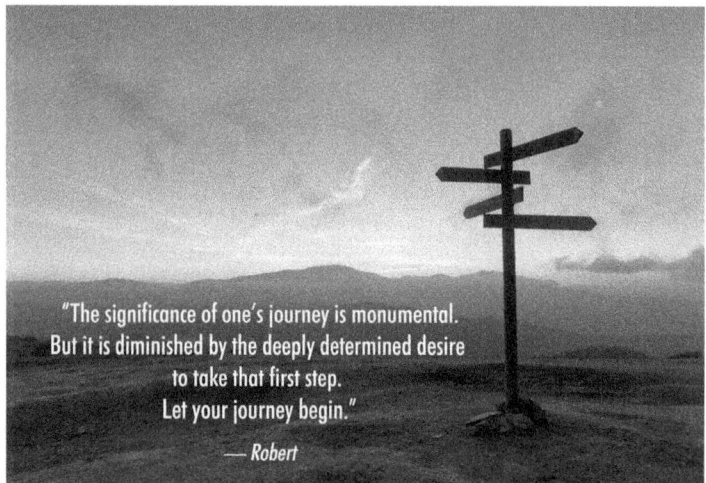

Photo Copyright © Mikel Martinez De Osaba

"An Ending Begins"

"Cats are smarter than dogs. You can't get eight cats to pull a sled through snow."

Jeff Valdez

LIKE NOAH, I LEARNED EVERYTHING COMES IN TWOS. You can't have an up without a down, a left without a right, love and understanding without conservatives, joy without sadness. So, with that thought in mind, I begin my adventures in "blogdom" by telling you about the loss of my beloved feline, Max.

Max lived life at his own nearly undetectable speed. Life would certainly never give him the bends. This is why I was so shocked when the vet diagnosed that he had a hyperactive thyroid. How a cat that lackadaisical could have a hyperactive anything was beyond me. I honestly don't believe Max was lazy. He merely had his own agenda, as any cat owner *(as if there really is such a creature)* can attest. Max had an attitude that screamed *"If it doesn't have to be done then don't do it…and if it does need to be done just let someone else do it for you."* Amen, little guy.

Max came to me 3 years and nearly 8 months ago through the friend of a friend. His arrival couldn't have been more ideal. I had just suffered a heart attack a couple of weeks earlier. I needed something else to focus on instead of myself. Max was a very cathartic blessing. He was more aloof than my earlier cats, VanGogh (yes, he had both ears) and Furball (yes you read that right), but he seemed to adjust to his new surroundings at his own pace. For the first month he lived under my bed only showing himself for meals and litter box breaks (for which I'm grateful let me tell you…). I would scoop him up in my arms, much to his furry chagrin, and attempt to make him feel safe. I swore to him, first and foremost, that I would never, under any circumstance, make him wear any sort of absurd creepy outfit. A cat has far too much dignity for such a thing.

Not to mention Max had claws and knew where I slept…

I dragged the poor guy from the heavenly surroundings of California to the world's largest litter box known as Arizona. After nearly three years there—and right around the time he'd almost forgiven me for the initial move into red dirt hell—I did it to him again. This time I yanked him to the east coast. And boy was he mad.

For the first half of the trek he refused to have anything to do with me. With my car fully loaded, he had the luxury of totally exclusive use of the passenger seat and floor. His cozy little bed was on the seat while his litter box remained on the floorboard. I told him to think of it as a split-level kitty RV (for the record he was unimpressed by the analogy). Max was so pissed off at me, in fact, that he opted to lounge in his litter box, the spot of the greatest distance between us, and not sit next to me. If that wasn't enough he even sat with his back to me! Cats can make a bold statement without meowing a syllable.

After taking a break for a couple of days with a friend in Dallas, Max mellowed out a bit. He spent the rest of the ride right behind my legs as I drove. Every once in a while I would glance down and see him with his paw on the brake pedal. "Dude," I said, "If I have to slam on the brakes you're gonna lose a paw!" That didn't seem to faze him. With Max it was all about control with minimal effort.

Everyone has a hobby. Max's happened to be shedding. He was exceptionally good at it so why wouldn't he want to flaunt it at every turn? After one day on the road the interior of my car appeared to be covered in wall-to-wall shag carpeting. My Matrix had turned into a four-wheeled mechanical Pig Pen, from **Peanuts** fame. If you touched the car you'd see puffs of fur spewing forth like a hairy hurricane. I was zipping through New Mexico with my window down. I thought it would be a great idea to roll down the passenger window to get a cross breeze going. So, the window went down and instantly a huge cloud of fur was sucked out on the already desolate New Mexico terrain. I'm convinced that if someone was driving behind me they would have called The Humane Society, thinking I had chucked my cat out the window!

At the ripe old age of 17 Max's system just wasn't what it used to be. He stopped eating within days of our arrival. He spent most of his time under my bed, as he did when he first came to me, or my drawing table. When I would be working he would make a point to slide under my chair where he would purr himself softly to sleep. I would reach down from time to time to scratch his head or his butt, depending on how he positioned himself. This seemed to ease his breathing a bit. I sprawled myself out on the floor next to him last night and, while stroking his head, I told him that if he needed to go it was OK. He did not have to stay for me. As much as I want him here I do not want him to suffer, which he clearly was. Who knew that this would be the one time he actually listened to me? In the wee hours of this morning, around 5am, Max took my advice and slipped away quietly. How can a cat both heal a heart and break it, too?

My trek east was at the same time as my move west in 1997. Max was born, I found out a few days after he passed, on the east coast. So we came full circle together. And, to be honest, I'm very uncertain of just how to go into the next stage without Max snoozing under my chair. I am comforted, however, that his love will always be with me. Yes, his loss is a tragedy in my life. But I can't fathom all I would have lost if I had never had him in my life at all. Hug your furry friends a little tighter tonight. You'll be glad you did.

I love you, Max. You're the best.

"It doesn't do to be sentimental about cats; the best ones don't respect you for it."

Susan Howatch

"Remember the Magic"

"Never worry about the size of your Christmas tree. In the eyes of children, they are all 30 feet tall."

Larry Wilde

TO THIS DAY I vividly recall barreling down the stairs on Christmas morning to discover a stuffed dog, sitting upright on a new sled, waiting with open paws just for me. Sure, the sled was cool, but that little beige dog captivated me. It was a Calvin and Hobbs moment. The dog was real to me and we were inseparable for years to come. He was the epitome of soft and cuddly. He had a music box in his back and, when some random adult would crank the wind-up key, my new sidekick would play a lullaby just for me. I would not go to bed without him clutched in an innocent death grip. And that is why, in my creative three-year-old logic, I had to name him 'Sleepy Dog.'

He was soothing and fuzzy and a most devout listener. He was a constant companion that I dragged around to so many places that he should have had his own passport. As time passed by my buddy started showing some wear and tear. His floppy ears were getting worn and thin. The poor fella even lost his nose in some freak unmentionable accident. My mother, carrying on the age-old tradition of parental plastic toy surgery, replaced it with a small blob of yellow yarn.

He fascinated me. So much, in fact, that I had no choice but to yank out his music box, too, ya know? How else could I learn what made my pal tick? It didn't occur to me that it wouldn't play once my experiments ceased. Thus began a life-long career of placing far too many carts way ahead of a vast number of horses. His tan coat was looking dingier over the years, too. He was, like the rest of us, aging. But his loyalty remained as solid as ever. That dog was my friend, my confidant and my sidekick on numerous adventures. And, yes, in case you're wondering, I still have him. The sled has long gone, as have the memories of many other Christmas gifts from that, as well as future, years. But 'Sleepy Dog' remains. I cannot imagine not having him or the magic he brought me. He was, and on many levels, still is as real as you and me.

This holiday season, and beyond, I hope you rediscover that magic within. Let it rise to the surface where you can scoop it up in your arms, embrace it and laugh with the unfaltering freedom as only a child can.

Some random boy with his grandparents, Christmas, 1964.

"The Range of Change"

"Growth means change and change involves risk, stepping from the known to the unknown."

George Shinn

A NEW YEAR is, as Queen Oprah says, "another chance for us to get it right." Resolutions are made, with full intent on accomplishing them, and then tossed aside within a month at best.

Why do you suppose that is? What is it that makes us slip into our old ratty sneakers instead of trying on a brand new pair of Chucks? Is it because we're just comfortable? Could it be that simple? Or are we just too lazy and too scared to try something new? We know we should lose weight but what's one more cupcake going to hurt? We know we should stop smoking but, come on, what's an occasional puff on the way to work in the morning? Sure, it would be ideal to spend more time on a treadmill and less time in front of the new plasma TV... but, damn, that TV cost a lot of money and I should use it as much as I can!

We're cowards. We're lazy. We're afraid of commitment. In other words, we're human. We constantly believe we really can get around to it tomorrow. Sadly, we don't always have that "one more day" guarantee. I've had more people than I can count come to me with those sentiments. And, just so you know, this concern comes from sitters as well as those in spirit. Hind sight is always sharp and clear but we need to get to the optometrist much earlier.

Don't waste your time making resolutions for the new year. Use your time to really think about what you want to achieve- not for a new year but for a new beginning, a new life, a new philosophy. Do you really want to exercise and eat right? Do you want to find a fulfilling career instead of just tolerating a job? Do you want to find love? Do you want this, that and the other? Then, as the shoe says, JUST DO IT! Oh, sure, we give it a shot for a few days or even weeks. But if you want change-true dye in the wool change-then you must stick with it. Change your routines and thought patterns. You need to take a new route, plan a different journey with a different map. If you keep doing the same things and the same things keep happening... well, you'll stay right where you are at a blinding rate.

Welcoming change is no biggie, folks. Embracing and implementing change is nothing short of huge. Don't let the positive changes you need pass you by. Reach out and grab that brass ring. And if you don't, just remember Sleepy Dog is watching you...

Happy New Year, kids. Cheers!

"FINDING YOUR PLACE WITHIN"

"Where do you go for direction? Don't bother answering because it's an absurd question. It's different for everyone. The importance is, from my own experiences, knowing that direction is being given. And, on some level, you are taking notes as you put one foot in front of the other. When someone tells you a joke do you sit and try to understand why the joke is being told or do you just laugh out of instinct? When you hear a sad story do you have to digest all aspects of it before opting for a response or do you automatically cry? You don't think, you feel. You are without knowing why and yet you accept it, yourself, as part of the package of life."

Excerpt from DAILIES by C. A. Filius

GUIDANCE IS A FUNNY THING. I often have clients come to me asking Spirit to hand over a step-by-step Playbook of their lives. Hey, who wouldn't love such a luxury? It removes the guesswork and allows us to cruise on autopilot. The electronic age has certainly provided a virtually endless supply of devices that have put our brains on hold. How many phone numbers do you have committed to memory?

"What's Frank's number?" you ask. "5!" they reply. Sorry, but speed-dial isn't always the best option.

We must–and I cannot stress this enough–participate in our own lives. We have to make decisions, we have to interact with others. There's no escaping it. It's OK to get stuck in traffic once-in-a-while. If anything it gives you a chance to slow down and take in your surroundings. You may be surprised at what you see. Don't waste your time taking all of the side streets because you cannot stand the idea of traffic congestion. Cruise the streets of your life and live! That's where your answers reside, you know? Within the fun of it all. If you're saying, "I don't know how to have fun!" then you should spend some time figuring out WHY instead of expecting someone, physical or spiritual, passing you a note in class. Term papers do not write themselves. Books do not read themselves. Hearts do not beat by themselves. Your passions—even the pursuit of them—are the fuel that you need. If 'regular' isn't giving you the mileage you want then it's time for an upgrade to 'premium,' don't you think?

You cannot be given the answer for you ARE the answer!

"Rejoicing Joyce"

"DO YOU HATE ME?" Those were the very first words my biological mother ever said to me. Talk about memorable. Do. You. Hate. Me.

I had already been warned of her sense of humor so, as my grip on the telephone receiver tightened oh-so-slightly, I quickly replied, "That depends. Are you rich?"

Joyce chuckled and answered, "No."

"Then I hate you," I said.

And we laughed. **Hard.**

Joyce and I marveled in the odd quirks that we shared. For example, we had a peculiar fascination with office supplies. We could easily spend hours in Office Depot just roaming the aisles like kids loose in a candy store. Oh, the simple joys of paperclips and hanging folders… We firmly believed that Little Debbie Oatmeal Crème Pies were the perfect food. And we also held to the belief there was nothing nearly as important, or necessary, as laughter. We had never encountered a situation that didn't scream for a joke. Of course, we couldn't guarantee anyone else would find something funny but, thankfully, that just didn't matter. Humor was the way to deal with most of our own tragedies. We saw it as a universal language and we were fluent in it. She was a painfully funny woman. My birthfather is, too, but in an entirely different vein. Joyce once told me that I was such a perfect meld of both of them that I could never deny them even if I wanted to.

When I attended my first family reunion I wore a t-shirt that read "Have your picture taken with the orphan! $5.00! Makes a great gift!" Joyce laughed so hard I thought she was going to fall out of her chair. Never wanting to be one to be outdone she demanded 50% of my profits. "If it weren't for my initial investment you'd have nothing!" she laughed. Can't argue with that logic.

She loved helping others. She was often donating time, as well as her exceptional baking skills, to anyone in need. This Joyce-Of-All-Trades would do anything from writing 'skits' for her church to helping her nursing home roommate with her hair. Whatever was needed. And it seemed like she was always baking a pie or cake for some sort of shindig or another. I once remarked, "You do a lot for people."

She smiled shyly and shrugged, "It's what you're supposed to do." Then she burst out laughing and said, "Besides, it gives me an excuse to taste-test the pies I make!" Did I mention we also shared an infectious sweet tooth?

Joyce had been in failing health for quite some time. In October of 2011, she lost her left leg to diabetes. She was blind in one eye and could barely see out of the other. To help protect that eye she would often wear a medicated eye patch. She told me, after her leg surgery, "Well, I have one leg and I'm wearing an eye patch. Looks like I have my Halloween costume all figured out!" I laughed until I cried. There's no doubt about it, Joyce had a hard life. But she faced it with a smile on her face, laughter in her heart and a pie or two within reach. Whether the pies were for eating or throwing is yet to be fully determined. My guess is it would depend on which would get the bigger laugh.

I exhausted the first 33 years of my life wondering about her. I spent nearly 10 of those years searching for her. And I was only able to share 18 years with her. For those of you keeping score that's the span of time measuring from birth until high school graduation. In the big scheme of things it's not even a fraction of the blinking of a bastard's eye. But I am blessed to have had that time with her. Every. Single. Second.

Joyce made sacrifices for me and my younger brother, Joe. She made choices that were not easy in the hopes of her 'lost boys' having better lives than she could possibly provide. If that sort of selflessness isn't being a mother then I don't know what is. And you cannot possibly hate that form of generosity. You hear me, Joyce?

She quietly passed, with little fanfare, on July 16th. I last spoke to Joyce the Tuesday before her passing. When I asked her what she was doing in the hospital she gave me an answer that was vintage Joyce. "You know me," she drawled. "I was bored at the nursing home and just wanted a change of scenery."

And we laughed. **Hard.**

How fitting that our last conversation, just as our first, evolved into a joke. Her first words to me spoke of self-imposed guilt. Her final words, "I love you," were those of self-acceptance and joy. Trust me when I tell you there was a lot of laughter in-between. And for that I am truly grateful.

"WE REMEMBER LOVE"

PRESIDENT CALVIN COOLIDGE once said, "Christmas is not a time nor a season, but a state of mind." I believe this sentiment should extend to Valentine's Day as well. I suppose it can seem a bit disheartening that we've had to establish a holiday to remind us to acknowledge love in our lives. One can, and probably will, argue that this particular holiday is manufactured solely for profit. It seems that Love has, like so many things, gone commercial. Well, duh. No PhD needed for that snippet of insight. But the essence of the day remains. Love is with us in so many forms and expressions. And, no matter what, we do remember it.

Have you ever forgotten your first love? Of course not. I certainly remember mine. That blonde Valerie Bertinelli doppelganger stole my heart lock, stock and barrel when I was 18. She was feisty, funny and she wore sarcasm like a second coat. No wonder we got along so well. She once filled out a customer comment card at a local pizza place entirely in French just because. What's not to love about that? I was young and stupid and head-over-heels.

I remember how I would get tongue-tied whenever she was around. I still recall the innocent euphoria of our first kiss. And God knows I vividly remember how she made me feel with just the sound of her voice. We were going to be together forever because, when you're 18, you know everything and every decision you make is not only brilliant but everlasting. I would, at this time, like to reiterate the whole "young and stupid" thing.

So, no, we weren't together forever. Big shock there. But I have never forgotten her or that time. Big things, little things, you name the size and form. I remember them all—especially on a soul level. I don't need Valentine's Day to remember her or to tell anyone that I love them. As we all know life can get in the way and the obvious will sometimes get shoved to the wayside. When that happens just take a moment and remember. If there's always room for Jell-O then there is always time to remind someone—even yourself—that you love them.

I often relay to my clients that if I could share any aspect of what I do with them it would be one thing and one thing only: the overwhelming sensation of pure love that comes from the Other Side. Our loved ones in spirit continually surround us in their unconditional love. And they would like nothing more than if we did the same with those on both sides of the veil. The best way I can describe how it feels to me is that it's a cross between a thousand baskets of kittens being shoved in the room and a Hallmark moment on steroids. It's pure and simple with an innocent intensity. It kinda reminds me of being young and stupid…

Take the time to tell those special people in your life that you love them. Family and friends, lovers and passersby. It doesn't matter. Like the shoes remind us, just do it. You may not remember it 20 years from now but I'm willing to bet those on the receiving end will.

"Carved In Stone"

"There is no moment or memory that is too small. Just take the time to allow the light to shine divinely and watch it all grow within your heart, your soul. This light will surely enhance even the smallest of gardens, providing you with shade and comfort from this day onward."

　　　　　　　　　　　　　　　　　　　　　　　　Robert

I HAVE ALWAYS HAD A LOVE OF CEMETERIES. If you know me, even slightly, then you know this little personal morsel. As a child, I would spy a graveyard from the confines of my grandfather's Buick and demand he stop the car so I could check it out. He would say, "But we don't know anyone buried there!" Oh, please. Like that was a credible reason. And, of course, he wouldn't stop. Grownups just didn't get me. To this day, if I spot a cemetery along any given route, I will stop and wander through for a bit. I cannot pinpoint my fixation to any solitary thing. I find them comforting and peaceful as well as just plain fascinating. Each and every resting place serves as slivers of living—pardon the fully intentional pun—history, brief glimpses into people you may not know but yet share a common element: mourning a loss. The grave often gives us a chance to reflect upon and celebrate the life of the person interred. I experience such warmth when I spot graves that are brightly decorated, often with random, yet very personal, bits and pieces.

I have seen final resting places decorated with everything from margarita glasses and Reese's Peanut Butter Cups to bottles of India Ink and cow-themed wind chimes. I've seen the small grave of a little one gone too soon blanketed with an array of their beloved toys. A grandfather's love of fishing was easily proven with a rod & reel attached to his headstone. The woman whose blatant love of casinos was shared in an epitaph, chiseled forever in granite, for all to see: 'I'd rather be in Vegas.' Tears of sadness and joy, mixed together, simultaneously grasping the loss while finding comfort in what made each person unique. How do you wish to be remembered? Words or actions? Collections or recollections? I'm sure you've guessed by now that I have a thought or two for my own…

Robert, my Master Guide, once described the physical life as a yardstick (apologies to my metric fans out there). "One's life covers allllll this space," he said, spreading his hands over the full three foot span. "And yet, when one has passed, so many only focus on this tiny sliver," he continued indicating the very end of the stick. "All that was measured prior cannot be forgotten. Do not permit the grief to block out the true evidence of the life lived and shared. It is all measured."

I understand the pain of loss. We all do. It is inevitable. And, frankly, you need to mourn, to grieve. Sadness, just as joy, is vital to the human experience. You cannot raise yourself above it for it is part of what makes you human. While the initial loss can be devastating we can often find comfort in the memories, allllll those other moments that filled the space prior to death, as Robert pointed out. While I deeply mourned the loss of a dear friend, I find myself, time and time again, recalling our last Thanksgiving together. It was nothing short of a modern retelling of a classic 1930's screwball comedy. That memory alone has carried me through some rough patches.

I find that Spirit often utilizes humor in their communications with us. Recalling a funny incident, relaying a comment that is "just so like them." It not only gives you evidence of their continued existence, but it also gives you inspiration to heal, move forward, and smile as you think about them. Some believe dealings with Spirit are to be solemn proceedings; void of what I feel is the true human touch. Sorry, but I disagree. Respond to them now as you did when they were here: with love and laughter.

"Don't Be Afraid of the Dark"

"I have been very blessed, right from the official beginning, to have a strong association with my Spirit Guides that is sparklingly crystal clear. Their personalities, like mine, are overwhelmingly strong, loud and undeniable. Ignoring them is just not a comfortable option. They command my attention when they have the need to speak. It greatly reminds me of a small child tugging on their father's shirt sleeve repeating, "Dad! Dad! Dad! Dad!" over and over and over. No matter what dear old dad is doing he eventually has to give in and scream, "WHAT?" When they request my undivided attention I have little to no choice but share their insight with others. I hope you're willing to listen..."

CAF

"THE MOUTH OF A CAVE LOOMS AHEAD, a gaping void along the side of a mountain of stone. It is monstrous in size, overwhelming to the visual senses. Ignoring its existence is futile, pointless. What steps do you take? You know not what awaits within its darkened walls. Other options are at your disposal, of course. You may walk around the expanding mountain range, searching for an easier approach. But what of its duration? Many cycles of sun and moon may, or may not, pass by prior to completion. You just do not know.

"You may wish to return from hence you came. Can you envision going back to where, and who, you were prior to this journey? Does this settle well and earnestly within?

"There is always the simplistic choice of merely staying where you are at this very moment. Contemplate the realization that this could be where you will forever take root. Look about you—is this where you will find nourishment? Contentment?

True Peace? Eternal Knowledge? Is THIS all you require for your physical incarnation, happiness, fulfillment?

"Stepping in the cavern of the unknown does not require courage, despite what you may think you want to believe. It simply requires faith—within and throughout—in yourself as well as whoever, whatever, you KNOW your Creator to Be. Step into the cave, Little One. And explore!

"You are far more aware, on a deeper soul level, that the mouth of the cave is presented for a reason. Worry not about the "why". Accept that there IS a "why" and it will be revealed—perhaps—at a future time.

"Do not toss aside precious, fleeting moments "finding" the courage to go within, Little One. There is no need for you ARE courage! Just as you ARE Love! Just as you ARE Light! Just as you ARE evidence of God's Own Divine Presence!
"The darkness will build around you as you dare to explore deeper within. The light in which you started will dissipate until it has faded from conscious view. And then what? Human instinct will bring fear to the forefront. You are lost, you fear. You are alone, abandoned. There is no hope in sight!

"But wait…are you not standing? You cannot see the cavern floor beneath you, but you FEEL it, do you not? Reach beyond yourself in order to feel the walls surrounding you. You are NOT encircled by nothingness. Are you of the unknowing mind that clings to the limitation of only seeing is believing? Travel beyond your limited senses, mindsets and crippling assumptions. See what is unseen. Live what seems unlivable. Allow the unknowing to remind you that acceptance does not require any knowledge.

"Take advantage of the darkness. Use this time to continually explore within. All the while accepting that the lack of surrounding light does not diminish the brightest of light that is your soul, your spirit, your being, your Creator within and throughout!"

The One Who Soars with Eagles

"Channeled On the Carpet"

"DON'T BE AFRAID TO HEAR YOUR OWN MIND."
My brow furrowed as I looked at the words scrawled on the paper before me. Both my head and hand tilted to the right like Nipper, the RCA Victor dog. "That can't be right," I thought. I took a deep breath and said, "Don't you mean SPEAK your own mind?" All I received in return was the raising of an ethereal eyebrow. It's amazing, isn't it? After all of these years I still question Robert. I like to think he admires my naturally inquisitive nature. Whoops. There goes that eyebrow again.

After a few moments, as if Robert was collecting his thoughts or counting to ten in order to refrain from slapping me in the back of the head, my pen-wielding hand dashed across the paper once more.

"If it is within your mind there IS a reason. There IS an origin. And it IS yours. Own it fully. Is it there to enhance? Is it there to educate, motivate, create or appreciate? Or is it merely caulking for a leaky, worn tub? Is it mental gibberish enabling your lack of focus? Does it hinder or heighten your life's path?"

And Robert gets peeved when I ask *him* questions? Then, correctly on cue, he delivered the truth right between the eyes: "Are your thoughts necessary or merely an excuse?"

Well, there's a question for the ages.

"Your thoughts can rule as well as be ruled. Like any skill, it requires time, true desire and total dedication. Only you can direct the flow of your own thoughts. You cannot rely on

Spirit to do this for you. What purpose, other than catering to your own laziness, would that serve? You are made aware of Spirit within your life in order to face physical challenges, trouble-free as well as taxing. Your freewill is not only the deciding factor but the action as well. It really is up to you. We merely shine the light, but it is "soul-ly" your option to observe.

"If you wish to clear the mind, cleanse the awareness of your Spirit, then sharpen your focus, your connection, as you would a blade… by keeping it to the grindstone! Work at it—with it—daily, not once-in-a-while or whenever the mood strikes. What if you exercised your body only when you felt like it? Can you imagine eating or bathing on the occasional whim? Why is it that you can easily set aside hours at a time to watch a series of television programs, to skim a magazine, or to catch the big game, but you will not take the required moments to connect with Spirit? I refer to not just Us, you know? I refer to You as well! Is a scoreboard more significant than keeping a tally of your own self-sight?

"Mock reality, whether presented to you or thrown at you, is truly nothing when it comes to your very own reality. Do not watch it—live it, own it, be it—for it IS yours. Why? Because it IS you!

"Again, do not be afraid to listen to the sound of your own mind. It will unquestionably reveal the truth within."

There was a pause—an unspoken 'think about that' moment. Then Robert's trademark, "I am done" echoed throughout the room and he was gone. My head jerked back with an exaggerated blink, the pen fell from my hand and rolled a couple of inches down the page. I exhaled heavily, as if I had been holding my breath, and I sat back in my chair. When Robert lectures me I often feel like I've been grounded and my allowance has been taken away.

But, of course, he was right. Distractions have been plentiful lately, to say the least. Admittedly, my birthday is always a season for such unfocused obsessions. I allow my mind to romp and frolic in the neighbor's yard giving absolutely no regard to the clearly posted KEEP OFF THE LAWN signs encased in rusty barbwire. One becomes illiterate when pandering to such notions.

I'm a control freak. I am the first to admit it. Robert's eloquent knee-to-the-gut made me realize my craving of control does extend beyond what I've thought…literally. One's thoughts can be organized and managed once you admit to WHY they are there in the first place. I can honestly say mine are there in order to keep from facing the next step, the ascending rung on the ladder. In the past I have often reflected on what I have not done, where I have not gone and other succulent shortcomings. Why am I convinced that introspection has to be negative? What about examining what I have done, where I have gone and, more excitedly, what I will do?

Listen to the thoughts within your own mind and, more importantly, give the one who put 'em there some respect. I'm gonna give it a shot and I urge you to do the same.

"A View Anew"

"When a person can no longer laugh at himself, it is time for others to laugh at him."

Thomas Stephen Szasz

I AM ALWAYS DISCOVERING SOMETHING NEW IN THIS WORK. It is honestly a never-ending tapestry woven with sometimes seemingly random threads. Odd color schemes, off the wall patterns, you name it. Yet, in the end, a beautiful image will reveal itself. The speed of the viewing goes directly hand-in-hand with my perception, of course. Like everyone, I will get caught up in the day-to-day choreography of life without taking notice of what is going on around, and especially, within me. That's usually when I fall flat on my face, as the revealing self portrait above can attest. My unmindful grace, spiritually and physically, can really only be compared to a herd of bulls in the midst of the worst bovine hiccup epidemic known to man while in a Faberge Egg museum during an earthquake. Twice. With my scattered thought patterns I am often bewildered on how I can actually do this work. Sure, I can talk to your deceased grandmother but, as of this writing, I haven't a clue where my keys are nestled.

Once I pick myself up off the pavement, piece by humiliated piece, I will review my own perspective. I don't make myself see things differently. Instead, I do my best to realize what IS. After all, it's my diverse outlook that caused the asphalt bellyflop in the first place. I rarely understand it right off the bat. But I take note and store it in the well-worn library in my head for a later epiphany. Yea, my self-perception is often different from how others, here and there, see it.

What I have been fascinated to discover is that the being in spirit that I connect with in a session will often times have a self-perception that greatly differs from the thoughts and/or memories of the sitter. Parents who feel they weren't there enough for their children while the child was perfectly content with them growing up. The spouse who wasn't as loving as he or she thought they should be while the one left behind couldn't have been happier. Over time I have realized that these differing views do not stem from an unhappy life or a self-deprecating existence. It comes from a heightened perspective in spirit of the truly limitless capacity of the spiritual heart. We can love until there is no tomorrow. Guaranteed. But, as I stated, getting caught up in the choreography of life momentarily distracts us. When I am told "I could have loved more" I see it not as a self-imposed fault but as a reminder to the sitter, "Love with every vibration of your being!" And, of course, pass it on.

Right now I would LOVE to know where those keys are…

"On Your Road Again"

"IT DOESN'T MATTER WHAT YOU WANT if you do not actively seek it! A wish upon a falling star, the dropping of a coin in a wishing well in a picturesque grotto, the rubbing of a rabbit's foot…all can be called symbolic but, in truth, it does not go beyond that! The falling star is beautiful to see, the tranquility of the grotto may bring you some peace, and the rabbit's foot is soft and gentle to the touch. Ya know what? Big deal. These sensations are fleeting, momentary only. Pursuit, active participation, will enable you to walk your path.

"Totems, symbolic articles as well as rituals, are, of course, useful PROVIDING you do not soul-ly rely on them alone. Your dream will not come to your door—you must venture out and rap on a few doors yourself. Mingle with the Universe, exchange ideas and ideals. Learn from the stumbles as well as the solidity of assured footedness! Your destined goals can be enabled, as well as disabled, by active AND inactive participation. Care to venture as to which goes with which?

"Look outside right now—outside your window as well as outside yourself—and what do you truly see? Stepping outside of yourself and gazing impartially within takes time and nerve—no doubt about that. But do it! DO IT! Do it again and again and again for it never gets old. Each gaze can provide new insight aligned within each and every moment of each and every step as well as hesitation.

"You know what you are made of, what kind of person you are, what your true aspirations are as well as the perspiration that goes into it all. Some days of travel are far worse than others. That is a fact of all Life. But, do you choose to dwell on that OR embrace the obvious that the opposite is true as well? How many vacations have you taken—from a single day to several weeks—where SOMETHING has gone awry? But, overall, you look back on it with joyous smiles and the feeling of a good time had by all. It may not have seemed all that grand at the moment, but hindsight and reflection are great tools in achieving clarity.

"The negative, the frustrations, the struggles are temporary. They will soon be overhauled by positivity and purpose. Providing, of course, that YOU do something to motivate it, as well as yourself, onward ever onward.

"Do it, my Children, whatever IT may be to you. Continue along your journey so you can beckon others to follow their own convictions and drive with a simple, yet powerful, 'Having a Wonderful Time! Wish You Were Here!'"

Thomas

"A Moment In Truth"

WHEN I TELL SOMEONE I'M A MEDIUM I receive a well-established array of responses. First and foremost is the slack-jawed blank stare that resides somewhere between disbelief and "WTF did you just say". That is usually followed by the religious zealot, who crosses themselves as they back out the door, insisting they'll pray for me but at a distance. A nearby neighbor is the flat-out skeptic that wouldn't believe Santa if the jolly old elf slapped 'em into a Christmas tree. And finally, you have the delightful souls who already know of the infinite possibilities and realities of what I do. It's those people who dowse me with an assortment of questions and commentary that would rival any Whitman's Sampler box of chocolates.

The most popular of these is, "You are SO lucky to have such a great gift!"

Most days I agree with that wholeheartedly. Lucky, blessed, honored, you name it. But there are times when this gift feels more like that gaudy, ill-fitting sweater that was knitted by your colorblind great aunt after nine too-many holiday eggnogs.

I will say, up front, that I have witnessed moments that can only be classified as miracles. I have seen lost faith restored, spiritual reunions from across the ethers, grieving parents embracing and accepting the continuance of the lives of their beloved children once thought gone forever. I have seen so many people sitting before me laughing tears of joy, instead of sorrow, as their loved ones brought those happy moments to the forefront once more. I've delivered guidance from a place higher than our own level of being. I have relayed messages far beyond my own understanding that have assisted others in healing, believing in themselves again, freeing themselves of self-imposed guilt or shame. Miracles. Each and every one.

But, as with anything, there is a downside. Those moments that rank right up there with getting a root canal at the DMV as your ex announces all of your shortcomings over the PA system all the while scraping their fingernails on a chalkboard. Get the idea?

There are quite a number of unforgettable slap-in-the-face annoyances. For example, there was the geriatric client taking a whiz in the midst of a phone reading. Yes, it could have been worse. She could have done it during an in-person session. I suppose I should count my blessings on that one. What got me, beyond the absurdity of the whole thing, was the blatant disrespect the sitter demonstrated for me, the process and, most of all, Spirit! Another kick in the gut are those who actually see no harm in asking me to "spy" on people for them. "What is my ex-husband doing right now?" Another fun one was, "How can I hide my property in Vail from my ex-wife?" Really, people?

I vividly recall a reading I gave in 2008. She was a divorcee and had recently reconnected with an old high school flame. They were going out on their first date in 15 years and she, in essence, wanted to know if she was going to get laid. Hand to God, that's what she was asking. I did not receive, nor did I search for, a response to that inquiry. I simply made myself available to whatever insight Spirit wished to pass along (such as a boot to the head, for example, but I digress). Spirit, never being One to disappoint, gave her something truly amazing. I found myself being visited by a young, fair-haired toddler, no more than two years of age, calling out to her 'mommy.' She was smiling, full of life and light, with arms outstretched as if coming in for a doozy of a hug. I described what I was sensing to the woman. And her reply shook me to my very core.

"Oh, yea, that's my daughter," she said. "She was hit by a car. I know she's OK. So, what about my date on Saturday?" She honestly could not have cared less. I still reel over that one. Where was her heart? Her soul? It was as if she was a gas tank well under E.

Those sessions are the ones that really knock me to my knees. The ones that make me question this life choice of mine. I was enraged and, yes, insulted. Insulted for not just myself, but for her daughter as well. How could the woman snub such a gift? After the call I just sat in my office fuming over the ordeal. And, as usual, my Master Guide, Robert, stepped up with his own gentle boot to MY head. Robert tends to be my voice of reason. Now there's a duty that can test the patience of even the highest of evolved souls.

Robert stated, "Everyone, and I mean every single soul, is an individual. Each soul has their own journey to undertake at their own speed and time-frame. You cannot permit yourself to be caught up within the placement of another along their way. You cannot be angered by the soul in front of you at the market just because you have 1 item and they have 1 times 20! They are doing as they see fit at that time, they are traversing at the rate they deem fit for themselves. They are accumulating what sustenance they require—IN THE MOMENT. But what about tomorrow, tonight, an hour from now? Minds change. Ideals renew. Beliefs destruct and are rebuilt. The city skyline changes, buildings rise, fall, alter…only to rise again. Judge not in the moment for you are unaware of what the next moment may bring. Give thanks for the moments—each one—and for your opportunity to witness all that it brings forth. Especially the limitless possibilities of unending renewal!" There was a brief pause and then his signature sign-off, "I am done."

Well, I guess he told me, huh? But Robert's right. He's always right (and you have no idea how often he holds THAT over my head…)

This work saddens me when I am faced with the cold-hard fact that there are many people feeling so lost, hopeless, even empty inside. But that sadness is replaced by the truth in Robert's memorandum. What may seem hopeless today can become hope tomorrow, tonight, an hour from now… even by the very next moment.

"One Ella of a Ride"

I TAKE GREAT PRIDE IN BEING THE PROBLEM CHILD under the rolling eyes of my disembodied caretakers. Robert, my Master Guide, has told me in no uncertain terms that I have driven him to drink. I'm convinced my Guides gather together in a pub on the Other Side and do nothing but complain about me. "Whose idea was it to start talking to him?" one will say. "It was so much quieter then!"

Yea, well, guess what? I wonder the same thing. Whose idea WAS it to start talking to me? I'm convinced They only connect with me for Their own entertainment. I am just a way for Them to pass the immeasurable hours.

I was first introduced to Robert within my second attempt at automatic writing. Laura, my Protector Guide, came in a few weeks later, as did Martin, my Life Guide. From time to time, I would sense something new in the air and a new Spirit Guide would join my already growing firm. The number finally rounded off at a nice even ten a few years back. I honestly figured that was the maximum room occupancy for this fiasco of a ride. Ten is a nice even, comfy little number. It's quite popular in rating scales and it's the core of the whole metric system. All was set in stone and I was snug as a bug in a rug with my Spiritual Entourage.

Or so I thought.

A few weeks ago I felt "it" again. I was vacuuming of all things (domestic God that I am) when I stopped in mid-glide. Turning off the vacuum, I looked around the room and I knew

I was not alone. And this wasn't one of my well-established peeps. Not by a long shot. I felt someone was circling me, slowly, assessing me with every step. "All right, who's there?" I'm known for my originality don'cha know? My radar darted about my surroundings as I felt eyes of some sort focused on me. "Yesssss?"

I felt someone say, "Listen."

My initial thought was a female energy. This would be refreshing for Laura and Pamela as they make up only twenty percent of my male dominated support team. I closed my eyes, took a deep breath, and heard "Ella." Short, sweet and to the matter-of-fact-point. My eyes popped open and the other eyes were no longer upon me. I sensed nothing else so I brought the vacuum back to life with a quick click of a switch. "Ella, huh?" I thought. "I'll take a side order of proof with that." The roar of the vacuum drowned out Their collective 'sigh'.

Like the menu at the Soup Plantation, the events didn't matter and it faded from my mind shortly afterwards. I just chalked it up to the aftermath of too much swirling dust clouds emitted from my Red Devil. Late one night, while being slapped around by one of my dominant bouts of insomnia, I caught one of my favorite movies, IMPACT, on TV. This 1946 film noir gem stars Brian Donlevy and Ella Raines. I was about 20 minutes into the movie when it hit me (I'm quick on the draw, aren't I?). "Too coincidental," I quipped. "I need something more." I envision my crew just standing in a semi-circle behind me shaking their heads in unison.

Admittedly, I am a bit of an Ella Raines fan. I've snagged a few photos of her over the years at some Hollywood memorabilia shows (yes, I am THAT big of a nerd). So the name Ella DOES have a personal significance for me. That being said, I'm thinking I could have easily allowed my own subconscious feed me the name in the beginning. My love of old movies would dictate that I would select an older film to watch at that hour. I pride myself in my logic—a polite word for 'bullheaded stubbornness'. Once the movie was over, and I was not even close to renewing my citizenship in Slumberland, I jumped on eBay and gave a cursory search for Ella Raines memorabilia. One of the first items up for bid was an autographed photo! Well, how about that? I've seen a few autographed pieces over the years and the bids are almost always nearing the triple digits. Too rich for my cholesterol tainted blood. But this photo was different. It was being offered at a mere $18.00. While the black and white photo itself is not one of her best, the signature was billed as being authentic. Upon inspection my heart stopped, started again, skipped a beat and then began to swing dance. The photo was endorsed, *"To Charles..."*

Yes, once the feeling came back to my brain, I bought it.

But, once again, I doubted. It's no wonder that I have a Guide named Thomas. Doubt is my Native American surname.

Later in the week someone on a Movie Memorabilia list to which I subscribe, posted a set of autographed photos he was selling. He was clearing out an enormous collection of photos from the Golden Age of Hollywood. I glanced over the treasures, ranging from Bacall to Ball and Cagney to Cotton, and found myself coveting each and every one. However, the only one that really jumped out at me was that of Colleen Moore. She was a popular actress in the 20's and 30's until her early retirement in 1934. I really knew nothing about her. I knew the name and that was about the extent of it. But I found her photo absolutely captivating. Honestly, there wasn't really anything special about it but, on some level, it spoke to me. I emailed the seller and asked for the price. I was told it was $50, non negotiable. Too much for me at this point but I just couldn't get the photo out of my mind. So, like any good geek, I started researching Ms. Moore. I wanted to find out why I found the portrait so enchanting. I soon discovered that her most famous role was in a 1926 modernization of Cinderella entitled "ELLA CINDERS."

Oh, come on… Seriously?

Like a dog with a really juicy steak bone, I began gnawing even more. It seems that Ella Raines and Colleen Moore were both born in the month of August. My spiritual journey began in August, 2001. Both women passed away in 1988, which is an "8" in numerology and, yes, kiddies, August is the 8th month.

But, yet again, I'm just not buying into it. (Yea, save it, I know what you're thinking…I am psychic after all!) I still hadn't felt anyone or anything since the drop-in while I was channeling my inner house frau some days prior. Oh, sure, I could have just taken the time to simply meditate and tune into this new energy but, c'mon! That would just be silly! In case you haven't noticed, I wear my pigheadedness like a letterman's jacket.

A couple of nights ago, when insomnia and I were once again having a staring contest, I indulged in one of my guilty pleasures by watching an episode of MYSTERIES & SCANDALS on YouTube. This was a 30-minute syndicated TV show that was produced in the late 90's. It made up of hokey reenactments and "investigations" into various Hollywood scandals throughout the years. And, thankfully, the vast majority of them are stockpiled on YouTube. I looked over the program listings and chose, for reasons unknown to me at the time, the episode devoted to the tragic murder of actor, Sal Mineo. I was never a fan. Like Colleen Moore, I didn't really know much about Sal. But this is the only episode I opted to watch that night. As I clicked 'play' I actually said aloud, "I have no idea why I'm watching this." I discovered the answer 4 minutes and 4 seconds into the video. It seems that one of Sal's earliest acting jobs was a guest role on what I'm sure was a riveting program entitled 'Janet Dean: Registered Nurse'. Television in the 50's was just so simplistic, wasn't it? The title character, Janet Dean, was played by none other than Ella Raines.

Oh, Sweet Mother…

I just sat there, nestled somewhere between numb and awe. Admittedly, I didn't want to believe that I had yet another Guide. It seems silly, I know. But I honestly did not want to face this all too looming reality. I'd dodged it for quite a few days by this time and I was hoping my agile footwork would help me evade the entire event. Eleven Guides? Good God...Eleven? I must be a lost cause to them so does that now make me a charity case? Ella is my eleventh Guide. My Guides frequently use the number eleven in their spiritual shorthand. It's like a "thumbs up" from the Other Side in my reference manual. That's when I realized Ella even has an 11 in her name... "Fine. You win," I laughed. I spread my arms wide, and said what I always say prior to giving a reading... "OK, let's do this!"

I sat at my desk, stilled myself—a rarity let me tell you—and Ella officially spoke through me, via paper and pen, for the very first time:

> "It is what it is but only if that is how you choose to leave it. Something is before you at all times—a task, a choice, a pathway to take or ignore. Analyze it to your heart's content but, ask yourself, is this part of your action, your solution, or is this another excuse to not move onward? You always know the truth but are you strong enough to admit it aloud to yourself? Anything can be improved upon, anything can be enhanced and extended beyond its original conception. If your completion of each level is done to your true satisfaction then it IS complete! If it is only reached in order to give the delusion of execution then you are living, breathing and being a LIE. Please be true to yourself, respect your potential, honor your capabilities and be the LIFE!"
>
> — ♥Ella

I can tell you she's going to be quite the taskmaster. She has an accent but I am not sure of the origin at this point. It may be British, possibly Irish or Scottish. Her diction is quite exaggerated to the point that she even rolls her "R's". Her voice projects with great self-assurance. Her strong presence makes me think she may have even been on the stage during a lifetime or two. It's going to be an interesting experience as we get to know one another.

I can't help but wonder, of course, just how long it's going to take me to drive Ella to drink…

"Keeping the Change"

EVERY NEIGHBORHOOD HAS A FIXTURE, a mascot of sorts who is always there, come rain or shine. It seems as if you can almost set your watch by their presence. It comes to a point when you're convinced, even illogically, that they have been there from the initial creation. And, in all probability, they will still be presiding over it all long after you're part of the sediment on which you are currently meandering. Silly, yes, but we know bursts of absurdity have flashed through our own minds on occasions past, so what's one more?

My childhood neighborhood staple was Mrs. Farley. She was a short, stocky woman who was a sauntering bundle of sweet quirkiness. Her hair, always pulled back in a bun, served as a battleground for streaks of brown and gray. It was always a coin toss as to which would dominate the playing field upon her head on any given day. Like many in the neighborhood, she had her own little vegetable garden in her tree lined backyard, laundry draped over a clothesline stretched between two maples, and her front and back porches were a second home to a multitude of flower boxes overrun by gangs of geraniums. Nothing out of the ordinary. Except, during the humid summer months, she would sit on her small back porch serenading the neighborhood with her accordion. Hand to God.

I spent many a night growing up watching fireflies dancing to Mrs. Farley's rendition of 'Edelweiss'. I often entertained myself by giving Mrs. Farley a thick accent so she'd sound like Mrs. Olson from the Folger's coffee commercials. It amused me... Admittedly, it doesn't take a very shiny object to entertain me at any given time.

I remember her vividly and fondly. To this day, I cannot hear an accordion, or even watch The Sound of Music, without thinking of Mrs. Farley channeling her inner Lawrence Welk. Since Mrs. Farley left us in the mid-70's, I've lived in seven states and more mostly urban dwellings than I care to list for fear of overloading my already fragile GPS. My surroundings—my life—has changed time and time again. It happens, you know?

Life goes on as it's prone to do. Neighborhoods change, and so do their not-so-eternal staples and landmarks, the things we think will be there forever. And, of course, so do we. Changes, temporary and permanent, are inevitable. It happens to us all, whether we like it or not. Take a long hard look at yourself right now. Are you the same person on the same levels as you were five years ago? Five weeks ago? In some cases even five days ago? Big and small, change is with us, flaunting itself like an egocentric peacock. "Look at me! Look at me!" But, you know what? The most earth-shattering change is the kind that sneaks up on us. The change that roosts high upon a limb, well above our inflating and/or deflating ego, cooing softly like a dove. Then, out of the blue and when you least expect it, it drops on you – SPLAT! It drops right on you and your classic '66 Mustang that you've been painstakingly detailing for the past four-and-a-half hours! It can make you realize that some of the things you thought were important were really no more than distracting filler. And, at the same time, you grasp that a few things you took for granted were a bit more significant than you once believed. Well, imagine that.

Have you noticed how much positive PR there is out there regarding hindsight? We all crave it, need it, covet it even. But we rarely have it until… well, you know. Once that reality hits, you suddenly become double jointed as you enthusiastically kick yourself in the butt over and over and over again. The battle cry of "shoulda, woulda, coulda" begins playing in our head like an annoying tune (the theme to the old **'Light Bright' commercials**, for example… you're humming it to yourself, aren't you? BWHAHAHAHAHA!).

There's a fixture in my Long Beach neighborhood who lives about two blocks from me. I see him virtually every single time I'm strolling through the vicinity. He's a larger man, bald with a large walrus-type mustache. His olive skin shows a lot of wear-and-tear yet his deep, dark eyes seem to sparkle. He sits in his wheelchair on the sidewalk outside of his apartment building either chatting with neighbors and anyone passing by or watching his portable DVD player. There is a small American flag hanging on the back of his chair proudly displayed next to a US Marine's decal. An ever present cigarette can be found lodged between his pudgy index and middle finger of either hand, giving the impression of being an accomplished ambidextrous smoker. No matter how warm and sunny it may be he is always bundled up in a heavy coat and knit hat. His obviously swollen feet are encased in heavy wool slippers. He speaks every time I pass him. His voice is strong, not intimidating, and genuinely friendly. When he asks, "How are you?" I honestly believe he is actually interested in whatever answer I provide. Our relationship is not a complex one by any means. It never strays from the usual generic pleasantries regarding the always topical weather, which is wedged between the verbal parentheses of "hello" and "see you later". We haven't even taken the time to introduce ourselves to one another. But, like clockwork, he is always there, come rain or shine. You can set your watch by him…if you're wearing one, that is.

That relationship altered greatly last week. I was walking my usual route when I came to his spot on the sidewalk. Instead of seeing him in his ever-present chair, I saw a large makeshift memorial. There were several candles—eleven in fact—and more than a few flowers. Attached to the gate was a large piece of cardboard covered in a wide array of handwritten sentiments. In the lower right hand corner of the cardboard was a United States Marine's decal. There was one photo displayed and, low and behold, it was him. I was stunned. His name, I discovered, was Richard. But nearly everyone referred to him as Taco. There were notes from a wide range of individuals. Clearly all very close friends who are deeply affected by the loss of their brother, their fellow journeyman, their buddy. The shaky, unstable printing of a young child was clearly visible, too, as was their own personal sense of loss. Taco's American flag, which was always present on the back of his chair, now looked down over it all from the upper left hand corner of the memorial.

I was shocked at how this man's death hit me. As I said, I didn't really know him. But he was familiar, he was a part of my surroundings, and suddenly he just wasn't. His exit was another all-too-present reminder of not only the brevity of our physical life, but to make a point to be a bit more interactive with our aforementioned surroundings. People, places, any combination thereof.

Change can knock your socks off. But, maybe that's just a sign that it's time to go barefoot for a while. A reminder to reconnect with your surroundings minus the filler, the distractions, the sentiment we often displace. Common sense dictates that if you lessen the load you can pick up the speed. The question is, what do you keep, what do you discard?

Ella, the newest member on my roster of Spirit Guides, offered a look into this quandary. She channeled the following with her usual iron-fisted finesse…

> "Let It Go! Let It Go! Let. It. GO!
>
> "Let go of what, you ask? Does it matter? What holds you down? What darkens your spirit, your soul, your heart? What heaviness burdens you down and impedes your speed, adding worthless weight when more substantial supplies are requisite? A car has four wheels so do you carry eight on your trip? You do not require the bare minimum but, instead, learn to bear the minimal. Discard what does not serve, carry what you need. Then be willing to remove along the way while embracing the replacements as they come forth.

> "Nothing stays the same forever. Your life path changes. Your attitudes and beliefs change, your friends and loves—they all change. What makes you believe that you are immune to change as well? Do you actually think you are above all of that? Flexibility, my child, flexibility. Flow as the river or come to rest in the debris of the dry riverbed. Nourish to flourish, starve to stay put. The choice is, of course, always yours."
>
> – ♥ Ella

We have been given this life so, my friends, make a point to actually LIVE IT! Don't just meander through its halls. Check each door as you go along, rattling the knobs of the ones currently locked, and then move on to the next. Different doors, different rooms, different surroundings…one change after another. Explore them. Some changes will work for you and some will not. That's just how it goes. But you won't know until you face them.

Allow the changes—no matter what they may be—to fuel, not hinder, you. A new job or someone's death are both changes. Initially, one seems a lot better than the other, right? But how do these changes truly affect you in the long haul? A new job brings with it great promise and potential. No complaints there! The loss of another brings sadness and sorrow. But, what about the change that follows the initial reaction? A loss can, in time, help you better appreciate what you've had, what you currently have and what you may have with others down the road. You see, there is even change within change. As Ella stated, "Nothing stays the same forever." And, believe it or not, that's a good thing.

So, Taco, I thank you for this change in my life at this moment. I thank you for the reminder to step back, regroup, rethink and reevaluate. If anyone reading this has an epiphany or two because of it, then make a point to thank Taco, too. You see? He may be physically gone but he is still speaking to anyone who passes by his way. And, if you run into Mrs. Farley, be sure to give her a "one more time!" from me.

"A Getaway is a Great Way to Stay"

"Laughter is an instant vacation."

Milton Berle

IT'S ALWAYS NICE TO GET AWAY, isn't it? It doesn't really matter if it's a short day trip, a weekend getaway or a full-blown two-week romp. Just having a chance to run away from it all to recharge the batteries is a blessing, a gift and, frankly, a bright shiny gold key to some resemblance of sanity. Where do you go to recollect yourself? Do you prefer to lounge on the beach with your toes burrowed into the granular mounds of sand separating you from the sprawling ocean before you? Maybe you're solace is found on the wooden porch of a cabin high in the mountains as you look out over a sentry of trees staring silently back at you. Whether it is the hustle bustle of Vegas, a day at Disneyland, or a few hours visiting with your grandmother—each and every one of us needs to get the heck outta Dodge from time to time.

I was fortunate enough to spend Memorial Day weekend in sunny San Diego. I was attending The National Cartoonists' Society annual Reuben Award weekend. The Reuben, in case you're wondering, is the cartooning equivalent of the Oscar. The only difference between the two is that no one really cares about the Reuben. In reality, it's a great excuse to spend time with fellow ink-slingers. Cartooning is, for the most part, a fiercely isolated profession — as if being a medium fills one's social calendar! This is nearly the only time we get to see one another—or anyone else for the most part—so we take full advantage of the opportunity. We spend hours hunched over a drawing table with nothing but the continual clicking of the deadline clock echoing inside our heads. So, getting the chance to actually talk to someone else is nothing short of euphoric. The most intimate relationship I have is the weekly drop off by my close personal friend, Whats-Her-Face, the FedEx girl. Yeah, we're tight.

I always have a great time at these yearly events but there was something special about this go-around. I completely let loose (now there's a scary thought!) and had more than my quota of fun and frivolity. As odd as it sounds, I was completely stunned at this fact. Normally, I am one to socialize a bit, hibernate a bit, socialize a bit, hibernate a bit, and so on. This time, however, the hibernation was deeply dwarfed by the socializing. This character was totally out of character. After a day-and-a-half I realized that I had been in dire need of this vacation and I hadn't even realized it.

It's a tad alarming when you suddenly recognize how out of touch you are with yourself. After all, you're with you 24/7. You really cannot escape it no matter how hard you try. Yet we tend to let ourselves slip by as we continually pile the daily duties and responsibilities higher and higher until we cannot see around them. We're blinded by them. What happens next? We accept the limited view that we've invited into being as our only reality. I often envision myself as the guy on Sesame Street carrying an armload of pastries announcing, at the top of a long flight of stairs, "Ten banana cream pies!" And then, unable to see where he is going, he falls down the mountain of steps leaving a funny trail of meringue and crust along the way. As a friend of mine used to say, "I'm hopelessly lost but making damn good time."

This point was driven home on my last night in San Diego. Our farewell soiree took place aboard the USS Midway. I have no clue who thought it would be perfectly safe to entrust a battleship to a bunch of overgrown adolescents, but that's beside the point. As I was walking aboard the massive vessel I told my Guides that I would be totally open to any Spirit Communication that there may be aboard. After all, I was walking onto a virtual piece of history! You just KNOW there are many impressions out and about on the sprawling decks. Spirit, as always, had a different agenda. My request was answered with a resonating "NO."

Admittedly, I was shocked at their response. Before I could question the reply I was told, "Just go and have FUN!" And, as God is my witness, They left. Every last one of 'em (and you know that took some time!) I wasn't there as a medium. I was there as a cartoonist, with my fellow brethren, left to my own devices. Not being one to disappoint my entourage too often—at least I hope I don't!—I continued relaxing, laughing and just having a grand old time.

Yes, it IS good to get away. It's even better when you're able to realize just how vital any form of rejuvenation really is. Life is life, pure and simple. Responsibilities and that thing they call reality will be with us for the long haul. But we need to take the time to listen to ourselves, our souls, and understand when it needs a break from it all. It doesn't matter if it's five days or five minutes, but you have to take the time to treat yourself. A meal, a trip, a walk to your favorite park. Indulge in that personal "me time". And if you're thinking that you have no idea what your "me time" is then that, my friend, is a cast-iron giveaway of just how badly you need it. Body and Spirit both need a time-out.

"Time is precious, just as you are. Both need to be respected, cultivated, cared for and fully realized. Precious moments connect one by one to create a lifetime. How sad it would be to have breaks and stops through this pathway, this life, that are not required. Enjoy this journey, this purpose, this time. Be good to yourself at all times so that being good to others shall come more readily, more easily, more naturally."

Laura

"Picture This"

MOST OF MY EXPERIENCES have begun with "…there I was, minding my own business when…" It is becoming my new age counterpart to "It was a dark and stormy night." Of course, if you know me, you will realize that's an ideal fit. So, here I sit, in the wee hours of a full moon, typing away atop my doghouse, projecting my thoughts for any eyes that care to peruse them.

I spent last Thursday freely wandering around LA, minding my own business (there it is!), when I dropped by an odd little shop on Melrose Avenue. It's an eclectic storefront catering to a far different mindset nowhere near the K-Mart crowd. It's the only place in town that I know of where you can purchase a tarot deck, a dog skull AND a Norman Rockwell print all under the same roof. And who among us hasn't had all three of those juicy morsels on our shopping list at one time or another?

The reason for my being there was to purchase a business card holder that happens to look like a small coffin. Yes, you read that right. I want to entice clients to pick up a business card by pulling it out of a slot in the top of a mini-casket. It would be a perfect companion piece to the delicately carved set of wooden hands that I currently use. It's a marvelous conversation starter—and sometimes stopper, depending on the timidity of the individual. Much to my chagrin, I was informed that the item I so desperately wanted was no longer in stock. Well, that's a fine how-do-you-do. To appease my disappointment I wandered around the curiosity shop, sulking, in hopes of finding one lone stray that the shopkeeper had long forgotten.

No such luck. Curse their flawless knowledge of their own inventory.

I did happen upon a box of old photographs, however. I'm talking old, turn of the century stuff. Black and white, sepia tones, even tintypes. Well, I'm a sucker for such oddities, so I naturally soared right to them like a hummingbird to a symposium on nectar addictions. I reached into the tray of the first box and I randomly pulled out a photo. It didn't take long for me to realize there was nothing random about it. I immediately did a double-take that would make Oliver Hardy proud. It was a photograph of a man wearing a dark three-piece suit. His tall, lanky frame is leaning against a tree, an arm draped through its fork, the other at his side, his hand clutching a bowler hat. You can see what appears to be a light colored mesh scarf of sorts draped over one of the limbs of the fork. He has a dark handlebar mustache, a prominent nose and intense, piercing eyes. The kind of eyes that can bore a hole right through you. His hair is parted in the middle and swept back on both sides. His face is square, his jaw firm. You can clearly see his pocket watch chain glistening in the light.

I gazed at him for a few moments in focused curiosity. Several years ago, I was given a description of my Master Guide, Robert, by two different—well technically, three—psychics. The first was Rita Berkowitz, the renowned psychic and spirit artist. The other was Terry & Linda Jamison, aka The Psychic Twins. The descriptions of Robert from these individuals were all but completely identical. I was told he was wearing a dark three piece suit, with a slim tie, of course. He was tall and thin. His nose was prominent and he sported a dark handlebar mustache and dark hair, parted in the middle and swept back. Both made a comment that he reminded them of an undertaker in the old west or the turn of the century. How ideal is THAT? The only difference was that Berkowitz said he had a square featured face and the Twins described his face as being long, oval shaped.

I have had glimpses, both physical and energetic, of all of my Spirit Guides with the exception of Robert. He's the one I connect with the most and, oddly, he's the one that is the biggest mystery. Whenever I inquire specifics about him, he merely replies, "That is not important." When I badger him about it, like any big whiner baby, he simply says, "My past is of no significance to your path, your growth." If I continue to hound him—and you KNOW I do—he just shuts up. Well, LA-DEE-FRIGGIN-DA.

But he had no problem showing himself off to Berkowitz and the Twins. OK, so they're all prettier than me. But, c'mon! We work together! Throw me a bone, here, will ya?

As I stood in that shop on Melrose I was almost convinced I was holding that very bone in my hand. Of course, being the professional Doubting Thomas that I am, I started to shrug it off as a big ol' coinky-dink. Hey, this type of attire, as well as fashion sense, was quite popular back in the day. I could have found any number of photos of men who resembled the one in this particular photograph. To appease my self-righteous arrogance, I quickly flipped through the other photos in the box. Low and behold, I did not come across a single photo of anyone looking like the fellow in the one I was clutching. I admit I was a bit surprised by my lack of discovery. I fanned the photo slightly, tapping its cardboard edge on the fingers of my left hand in an odd out-of-step rhythm. The sound was internally deafening while virtually inaudible to anyone else. "Weird," was all I could mutter to myself. Without thinking—which really is pretty customary for me in most situations—I flipped the photo over. While having no scientific proof of this, I am all but convinced that my eyes suddenly resembled saucers that consumed the greater part of my face.

Scrawled on the back of the photo was a name and nothing more: Robert King Brown.

In my natural, nearly deafening voice, I simply said, "Holy shit." While not the most spiritual of quotes, I defy you to find one more honest or sincere.

Admittedly, I am not one who can just leave things alone. No matter how blatantly obvious something may be I have to dig just a little bit deeper. No worries. My people know that and I'm convinced that's why I always uncover a few remaining gold nuggets from what most would think is a tapped vein. There are 15 letters in the gentleman's name. That totals a six in numerology and, of course, I'm a six. Impressive? Sure. But the real kicker is that his full name in numerology totals an eleven. My Guides have used this number as a "thumbs up, it's all good" sign from virtually day one. Eleven is a Master Number. It's a biggie as many of you know. It's all about spiritual enlightenment and the ability to make that enlightenment a reality in the material world. For example, materializing what may very well be an actual photographic representation of one's own Spirit Guide.

I've preached this a thousand times, and I'm sure I will preach it until I can preach no more: Trust. This work is all about trust. Trusting what you receive, what you sense, what you are given. And then continuing by trusting yourself to deliver what you've received, sensed and, yes, been given. And the reason I scream it from the rooftops with such determination? Because, like so many, I am just not embracing my own message. "Do as I say, not as I do" is NOT a mantra to be flaunted. It's about as de-motivational as you can get. It's like a distorted reflection in a fun-house mirror. You do have the image but it's no truer than the BS you cling to with false hope and misguided intentions.

I've made great pains to ensure I deliver what I'm seeing on the screen in my head. I do my best to not sugarcoat or edit. But often times I am bewildered by whatever is before me so I commit the ultimate sin: I think. Oh, when will I learn? Thinking will get you in trouble every time. When I am being shown a tacky orange and green ashtray then I need to just blurt it out. When I am insistently told to not give up on someone then, by jumpin' Jehoshaphat, do as they say. Stop questioning, start accepting and just trust. Let go of the how, and know there is always a reason. A reason, I may add, that may not make a lick of sense at the time...and that's OK because you are trusting that the outcome will be as it is supposed to be.

So, thank you, Robert. I am humbled by your efforts. I can only pray you are getting paid overtime for things like this. I hope this will help each of you to not only be more trusting of how your own system is wired, but how you honor each and every surge that runs through it. Are you truly acting on your own better judgments and instincts with people and situations? Or are you going through the motions the way you assume others would prefer? It takes time and that infernal patience thing you hear so much about in order to get into a state of trust. I know firsthand that when you stray away from that mindset you will probably get one humdinger of a slap in the back of the head in order to set your inner GPS due North.

Onward, ever onward.

"Gabriel's Flight"

"Coincidence is God's way of remaining anonymous."

Albert Einstein

I LOVE TO TRAVEL. I always have. I'm never really happier than when I have an airplane strapped to my butt. As much as I adore be-bopping around the country, the only thing that makes me happier is being left completely alone as I do it. I have less than zero tolerance for chatty cabin companions on planes or trains. Just because we share a seat does not mean we're going to bond, become Facebook Friends or swap thrilling anecdotes of adventures in coupon clipping.

There are, of course, exceptions to this rule. For example, several years ago on a flight out of San Diego, I found myself sitting next to a monk. An honest-to-Buddha-Monk decked out in full monk regalia. When God hands you a plate of cookies it is just rude to pass on it. I found myself uncharacteristically turning to my seat companion and saying, "So, what do YOU do?"

He looked at me for a moment blankly then burst out laughing. Another off my bucket list: Make a Monk laugh. Check.

I was making my way to my gate at LAX for my recent trek to Wisconsin, via Chicago, when I first spotted him. A bald man, slightly under my own six foot stature, clutching a large See's Candy bag. "Ah-ha!" I thought to myself. "TOURIST!" He was clearly taking a large batch of various chocolate morsels for his family back home. I've noticed over the years that locals stuff their candy in their bags while tourists tend to flaunt their sugary trophy. I chortled at my nearly Sherlockian reasoning and ventured on to my gate. Once I secured a seat next to the closest electrical outlet—a highly coveted spot in any airport—I noticed See's Man standing nearby. Seems I was sharing airspace with a tourist from the Windy City. How funny that I would spot him upon my arrival at LAX. What are the chances? I mean, out of all the airlines and gates and terminals at LAX I spot, almost the second I arrive, a guy going on the same flight as my own. Weird. I returned my nose to my book and happily tuned out the world around me.

I piled onto the plane with the rest of the herd all the while praying to any available Deity that I would avoid anyone even slightly enthusiastic about swapping verbs and pronouns. I made my way to my seat in the rear of the plane (seems fitting, doesn't it?), slid into my adored window seat and then just waited. People kept filing on-board as I kept shooting small, unobtrusive death rays from my eyes at each and every one of them. It was working. No one was sitting in my row. Hooray. The boarding was nearly complete and I felt I could let my guard down. I sank into the nearly comfortable seat, sighed a self-praising relief, while whipping out my customary bag of Peanut M&M's. Then it happened… One last straggler, panting, made a nearly Kramer-esque entrance onto the plane. It was none other than See's Man. He made his way happily to the back of the plane, smiling at everyone who met his green-eyed gaze. "No…no…no," I kept whispering to myself because, at this point, even my Guides aren't listening to me. He stopped at MY row, took off his coat, and stuffed it overhead. He slid himself into the aisle seat, leaving an empty space between us as his treasure trove of See's Candy went snugly under the seat in front of him. "Oh, just friggin' peachy. He's going to be friendly. I can tell…" I grumbled to myself.

He sat down, turned to me and gave me the renowned manly non-committal, "Hey."

I returned the same all the while tightening my grip on my M&M's. He was then kind enough to sit there and not say another word for over 4 hours. God love him.

The plane safely touched down in Chicago. See's Man, and his coat and bag, ventured off the plane following another emotionless "hey" exchange. All is well and right in my world once again. I wandered off to my next gate with the same determination I have as I circle the Lo Mein bin at any Chinese Buffet. My gate companions and I streamed our way onto the Wisconsin bound aircraft in an almost Pavlovian-like ritual. My seat was, thankfully, a single one on the left side of the plane. There was absolutely no chance of anyone even thinking of starting a conversation with me this time around. Life is good…

Then I heard a voice. "Hey! You again!"

I glanced up and, by God Almighty, I'm facing See's Man yet again! My eyes widened behind my tinted lenses as I said, "Seriously?" He just laughed and jutted his hand out to me. Well, I had to shake it or hand him my second bag of M&M's. Since I don't share, I went through the motions of being oh-so-gosh-darn friendly. We chuckled, one of us with sincerity, and he walked on by. Again…what are the chances of this happening? I stared out the window, asking my Guides, "What IS the significance of this?", as I gnawed on a mutant two-fused-as-one light blue M&M. I got nothing. So, I just shrugged it off. There were, after all, M&M's to explore.

I was standing in baggage claim playing luggage roulette by the carousel. Will my bag be within the first ten? Odd? Even? Who's to say? I fill my time with weird shit. No doubt about it. I glanced over my left shoulder and low-and-behold, See's Man was approaching me. I just looked at him, as he smiled, and said in my subtle, cellophane melting voice, "STOP FOLLOWING ME!" He laughed. He thought I was kidding. How adorable.

"So," I said, realizing he was just not going to walk on by, "Come here often?"

He smiled, "I'm moving here."

"Willingly?" I asked out of true bewilderment. "You DO realize they have REAL winters here, right?" The only way Californians realize it's winter is when we have sudden urges to wear socks.

"Yea. I know it's going to be different but I like it." He placed his See's bag on the ground and extended his hand yet again. (I thought we'd already finished with this ritual!) "My name is Gabriel," he said with genuine Midwestern sincerity.

I just smiled to myself and said, "Charles. Nice to meet you." When in Rome, you know?

We chatted a few more minutes until my suitcase finally made its curtain call. I snatched it up and wished him well in his new life.

"God's speed," Gabriel (aka See's Man) said as I hauled my American Tourister down the corridor.

As I made my way to the outside Wisconsin air, I thought it was pretty cool that I had an angel traveling with me. I figured it was just my peeps letting me know they were there. Awesome. I made a note to jot this down for a later date and then went on my merry way assuming that was the end of the story.

Assuming is, of course, the working word here.

Mediumship is, by no means, an exact science. Once the barn doors are open any and all animals within no longer feel a need to remain in their stalls. I may give a reading to someone hoping to hear from their loved ones when, out of the blue, a co-worker's father-in-law may make a cameo appearance. This has happened far more times than I can count. This has nothing to do with my inability to add—I am just far too lazy to actually keep track.

I stayed at the home of Gregg & Dar, both clients and now dear friends. Yea, I question their tastes in friends, too. I just assume it's based on pity. ANYWAY... During a reading for Dar last July I was faced with someone who was not in her own inner circle. The son of one of her high school friend's dropped by to reach out to his grieving father. Outside of a few snippets of information, Dar wasn't really able to confirm much of what the boy was giving me. She made notes of all that was brought forth and promised to later relay it to her friend. I provided her with a separate MP3 recording of his messages for his father as well. She contacted her friend who seemed somewhat intrigued but, as with many unfamiliar with the truth of mediumship, he was hesitant. He said he would get back to her once he made a decision. A couple of times afterwards he contacted Dar about possibly swinging by to hear it. However, on both occasions, their schedules just did not line up.

Flash forward to my October arrival. I doubt I had even been there an hour when, out of the blue, the man called and wanted to hear the barely 10 minute recording.

"Charles is here right now!" Dar exclaimed. "When do you want to come over?"

"Five minutes. I'm just down the street," he replied. Sounds like one of those so-called coincidences, doesn't it?

Through tears he was able to validate all of the information that came through via his son's never ending love. In the midst of this emotional roller coaster, he made an off the cuff reference to his grandson, Gabriel.

I just stared at him. You have GOT to be kidding me...

Moments later I received a text message from a friend of mine in LA. He was telling me he'd just spent the day in the San Gabriel Mountains. He makes frequent visits there but, in the past, he has always referred to it as simply, "the mountains." As in, "I'm going to THE MOUNTAINS" or "I really need to plan another trip to THE MOUNTAINS." I have never known him to refer to them as the San Gabriel Mountains. Well, go figure.

After Dar's friend left, I returned to my room to unpack. As I was mulling over this whole Gabriel scenario, I pulled my Archangel Tarot Deck from my bag. I was immediately given the short and sweet suggestion, "Look at the top card."

Since I have no will power of my own anymore, I removed the thick deck from its box and flipped over the top card. It was an Archangel Raphael card. I shrugged. "Yea? So?"

Then I heard this exasperated voice whisper, "No. The OTHER top."

Clearly the Angels feel the top of the cards should be the side with the angel's picture and NOT the 'back' of the card. So, I flipped the deck over and dealt from what was once thought of as the bottom. It was an Eight of Gabriel. My shrug was now replaced with slowly widening eyes. For hoots and giggles I checked out the very next card: The Nine of Gabriel. To add just one more cherry on the proverbial Sundae, I was told to cut the deck. I did without hesitation and found myself staring at The Page of Gabriel.

It was at that moment that my jaw and the floor fused as one. This was more than Spirit letting me know they were with me on this journey. But, for the life of me, I had no clue as to what it meant or what was coming. Some psychic I am.

My second group demonstration of the week was held at Kindred Spirit Books in Stevens Point. (Happy to make a shameless plug for this wonderful store!) The second reading of the evening went to two ladies in attendance, mother and daughter. The Spirit drilling through with an absolutely hysterical personality was the daughter's fiancé. He had passed tragically too soon in a vehicular accident on Mother's Day of this year. His energy was nothing short of dynamic. His humor and love was so vivid! His energy seemed to grow with each validation that was given. His fiancé and her mother were laughing through their tears, just as it should be. The healing truly excels once the tears of loss are replaced by those of recollection and love.

In the midst of this intensity he told me to stick my tongue out at them. Isn't it great that I can pull all sorts of immature stunts like that and blame it on the dead? I love my job, but I digress. So, like an obedient medium, I stuck my tongue out at the ladies. There was a brief gasp of shock and then they both laughed so hard I thought they would fall out of their seats. They explained to me that he stuck his tongue out in nearly every single photo that was ever taken of him. His mother-in-law-to-be said, "We have more pictures of him with his tongue OUT instead of IN!"

His fiancé laughed, wiping a tear from her eye, and said, "That is just SO Gabriel!"

I stared at her. It was if time had literally stopped. "Did you just say his name is Gabriel?"

She nodded, "Yes."

I was dumbstruck—emphasis on 'dumb'. Unbelievable. I took a moment and told them the whole Gabriel story. I finished by saying, "That guy has been hanging with me since I left LA! He's determined!"

His fiancé confirmed that. "You bet he was!"

Her mother added, "Honestly, on the way over here, I told her that with Gabriel's personality, it would be likely that he would show up first!"

"I'll be honest with you," I said. "The way he felt in the beginning made me sense he was actually late for the demo tonight."

Both ladies laughed again.

"He was late to everything," said his fiancé. "I even told him he'd be late to his own funeral!"

A group guffaw erupted on that one.

This is a grand example of how our loved ones are not only with us, but they are with others, too! Gabriel didn't know me from Adam, coincidentally the name of the son of Dar's friend mentioned earlier, but yet he knew I was on my way. He knew his beloved was going to be there. And, most importantly, he knew he could trust me with this responsibility and, for that, I am honored. Our loved ones, just as the love we share with them, know no limits or boundaries. There are absolutely no time or space restraints on our connections with one another. We just keep going and going and going, never ending, always loving and living.

I've always said that once this work bores me, when I am no longer amazed or intrigued by it, I will just walk away. Well, kids, I can honestly say I just can't see that ever happening. I hope Robert and the Crew are OK with that.

"The Impact of Brevity"

ON NOVEMBER 19, 1968, my mother, her friend Madeline and I were out for the day. Well, they were out and about for the day and I was dragged along because, like any 7 year old, I had no choice in the matter. The M&M's, Mom & Madeline, sat on the front seat of Mom's white Chevy Impala, with my mother's usual death grip on the steering wheel. I lodged myself just below the lone radio speaker awkwardly implanted in the middle of the back seat. Every time she'd hit a pothole the back of my head would bounce on the hard plastic speaker casing and I would just giggle to myself. That explains a lot if you think about it… I wasn't wearing a seat belt because it was the 60's and seat belts were more decorative than anything else in those days. It was a unique era. Smoking was still oh-so-very-cool, cat-eye glasses were all the rage, Adorn Hair Spray was best bought in bulk and seat belts were just a quaint fad that would go, one would assume, the way of Stretch Armstrong and the Kodak Flash Cube. Jeez, I'm showing my age.

ANYWAY…

For whatever reason, we ended up at the home of friends of Madeline's. The brood consisted of a husband, wife, and a passel of kids. The husband worked the night shift as a coal miner at the Farmington Number 9 Mine. I played with the other kids as the mom played hostess to Madeline and my mother. At one point, while nursing a glass of milk (my drink of choice in those days), I walked into the family living room and saw the dad resting on the sofa. The TV was on but he wasn't facing it. He was dressed in his work clothes, his feet clad in heavy light colored socks, and his work boots were placed neatly on the floor by the plaid sofa. He lifted his head, smiled and said, "Hi" to me. I responded in same and toddled out of the room. I was clearly the same engaging conversationalist at that age as I am now...

One of the kids, over the course of the evening, gave me a silly football player doll-like-thing. It was about 9" tall, lean & lanky with totally flat feet. It was encased in a soft cloth uniform supported by a flimsy internal wire skeletal frame which allowed me to bend him into absurd positions, sort of like Gumby. It couldn't stand on its own. I don't even remember why they gave it to me. I assume they found it as useless as I did, so they dumped it onto some unsuspecting kid as punishment for guzzling their milk.

In the early hours of the next day, November 20, the Farmington #9 Mine blew up. It was worst mine disaster in the state and one of the worst in the country. The explosion was felt where I lived, in a town about 12 miles away. I remember our house shaking in the wake of the blast, the windows rattling in unison. 99 miners were initially inside. They managed to rescue 21 but 78 were lost. The man I saw resting on his sofa was one of those who perished. This tragedy occurred in 1968 but his body was not recovered until 1972. There are approximately 19 still entombed in the old shafts.

I still have that football player doll. I would never want to part with it. That moment in time truly hit me hard. I only saw the man for a brief minute but I can still remember him in vivid detail. Whenever I hear of a mine disaster anywhere in the world my mind flashes back to that night and that man. The speed in which a life can be taken is a solemn reminder of the brevity of it all. Life can be staggering and overwhelming at times. No doubt about that. We have to remember that, no matter what, life is a precious gift. It may not always seem that way, of course. There are days when you're handed a stupid football figure but, when some time passes, you realize it can still be cherished even among the tragedies. My recommendation? Embrace it all.

"Savoring It"

"Christmas... that magic blanket that wraps itself about us, that something so intangible that it is like a fragrance. It may weave a spell of nostalgia. Christmas may be a day of feasting, or of prayer, but always it will be a day of remembrance...a day in which we think of everything we have ever loved."

Augusta E. Rundell

'TIS THE SEASON, OR SO I'M TOLD. I didn't receive this announcement via the Town Crier or a band of bubbly Carolers. It's the Retailers, accosting us door-to-door with their singing circulars, laying claim to the origin of this ideology. They have been preaching the Joys of the Glory of the Season for not only too long but far too soon. I find it a bit overwhelming to wander into a store when summer is still romancing us with beaches and barbeques, only to discover Christmas has already thrown up all over aisle four. Seeing pipe-cleaner trees and the plastic head of a decapitated Rudolf, when I should be eyeing beach blanket bingo cards, does nothing for my already weakened sense of reality.

It is said that the Great Wall of China can be seen from space. While not documented, I am convinced that my neighbor's home, three blocks down, is just as noticeable. The two-story brick & mortar Vegas Strip Wannabe is a sight best left unseen. Someone really needs to explain to the Home Dwellers that "gaudy" does not refer to anything of a spiritual nature. Every single palm tree surrounding the home is wrapped tightly in multi-colored lights. The dwellers of this electrical Partridge Family Bus clearly loved this stroke of engineering genius so much that they applied the same fetching theme to the posts along the front porch, the mailbox post and even the little wooden fence separating the lawn from any leering passersby. In fact, no slim vertical objects were safe from being encased in those little tiny florescent pokes in the eye. God forbid a lean, lanky telephone repairman would innocently happen upon this place. One can only shudder at his inevitable fate. And, God save us, all of the lights blink. Ouch.

The once normal front lawn now plays host to an inflatable colony consisting of a far-too-larger-than-life Grinch, Frosty the Snowman trapped inside of a snow globe, two largely distorted gift-wrapped boxes and something that I believe is supposed to be either an elf of an anorexic Cabbage Patch Doll. The individual motors join together as one off-key grating, chugging hum. The Grinch bobs to and fro as if trying to escape what I'm sure is hopeless humiliation. The large abstract packages reach for one another, like an old pair of windshield wipers, to only be jerked back in the opposite direction once more. The scrawny Cabbage Elf Thing seems like an afterthought. He's peering around one of the brightly colored boxes as if praying no one he knows spots him. The one that really freaks me out, however, is Frosty. Here you have a snowman trapped in a large snow globe. In essence, he is being bombarded with bits and pieces of snowmen that, in all probability, he knew. Creepy. And, on the porch roof, there's an inflatable Santa flying an airplane. One can only assume he's planning on dive-bombing on the atrocities below.

The entire frame structure of the house is lined in lights. Running, blinking, winking lights. Strands of green flashing bulbs are stretched and tangled within the shrubbery lining the porch. Ribbons snake in and out of the handrails. Two large Nutcracker Soldiers are guarding each side of the front door, scaring away any potential call from Avon. A large silver tree, covered in blue bulbs, stands tall within the frame of the main window. A multi-colored rotating light somewhere out of public view gives me the impression the tree is going through a barrage of radical and rapid mood swings.

To paraphrase, "This isn't what Christmas is all about, Charlie Brown."

I've always been a believer in the adage, "Less is more." Of course, that's pretty funny coming from someone as over-the-top as I am, but that's for minds far greater than ours to sort through at a later date. My eyes are always drawn to the delicate, subtle touches. The small home with a lone candle in the window, a diminutive wreath upon the door, the hint of a humble tree peeking through some lace curtains. Something done or given with genuine warmth and sincerity means so much more, don't you think?

My taste in shirts in the early 80's was a mere glimpse into what was coming down the pike…

My second cousin, Blanche, had a larger than life and, at times, abrasive personality. (This isn't the time to analyze family traits, either…) She wasn't exactly 'for just anybody.' Like me, you liked her or you didn't. There was no middle ground when it came to her. I found her wickedly funny. She shot from the hip, made no qualms of who she was, and lived her life with a very clear idea of what was right and what wasn't.

Blanche, a spinster, didn't have much in a monetary sense. She sewed quilts to provide for herself. And, let me tell you, her quilts were quite the prize! She did beautiful work. Word of mouth brought her work as she needed it. Of course, she wasn't overflowing with work. But she had enough to get by. She was a true artisan. Not quite the starving artist but meals could be skimpy from time to time. That is, of course, the time when family and friends would help out. One's hand reaches for another in need and so on and so on. You get the idea.

Every Christmas we could count on the same present from Blanche. One could set their watch by the welcomed predictability. Each and every year, instead of joining the masses and ordering from catalogues and standing in line at a department store, Blanche would bake homemade Christmas cookies. She filled tins that had once imprisoned countless fruitcakes with her cookies. Honestly, they melted in your mouth. I'm assuming they were nothing but two-thirds butter and one-third sugar. She cut them in the usual holiday shapes: stars, trees and bells. She heavily sprinkled them with red and green sanding sugar—she didn't slouch on the ingredients by any means. One bite and you could actually hear the granules of sugar crunching between your molars, much to the chagrin of dentists everywhere. Like her quilts, her cookies were top notch and done right.

Some would say, "Well, that's all she could afford to give" and just gloss over it. They would be prone to turn away and focus on something else like new clothes, hundred dollar sneakers, or the electronic gadget of the moment. You know what? I've lived through 53 Christmases already and, in all honesty, Blanche's cookies stand out ahead of so many other things that I've seen under the tree. Sure, it probably was all she could afford. But, the thing is, she was giving the best. HER best. It came from her heart, her kitchen, her very being. It was a part of her. She shared herself, her blessings, with her family and friends in a very personal way. We should all be so lucky.

Give of yourself, for the betterment of all, this Christmas and each moment afterwards. Then just sit back, prop your feet up, and have a cookie or two. You've not only earned it but you'll know to cherish every…single…bite.

Merry Christmas.

"Ruth's Rainbow"

MY MOTHER HONESTLY SAVES PRETTY MUCH EVERYTHING. Asking her to part with a pack of shoestrings or a mismatched handful of thumbtacks is the equivalent of spontaneously listing the highlights of the presidential administration of Millard Fillmore: It's a noble and even challenging endeavor but it's just not gonna happen. "I'll be able to use that one of these days," she'll say. So the item is filed away again until some yet undetermined later date when a use can be found. While not proven, I am fairly confident that Amelia Earhart's plane is tucked away somewhere in the back of my mother's hall closet.

While rummaging through a few boxes my mother had tucked away for some future archeologist, I recently found the remnants of one of my first grade art projects. It was a large sheet of manila paper, now yellowed and brittle with age (much like myself, whereas I've gotten fatter and the sheet of paper seems to be the same size). I had cut two pictures of a car, front and rear views, from some long forgotten magazine and glued them on the piece. The front view, over the years, had fallen off and gone on its merry way, leaving only an ancient dried glue Rorschach test in its place. A band of blue sky was scribbled in crayon across the top of the sheet, a blazing yellow sun beaming from one corner. The empty space between the blue sky and the cars was dotted with a healthy dose of "M" birds in a rainbow of Crayola colors. Beneath it, in shaky crayon, I scrawled:

> I like to go places in the car.
> We go to Bridgeport to my
> Aunt Ruth and Uncle Willie's house.
> Her grayam cracker pie is the best.

Dorothy Parker moved down a chair as I laid claim to my rightful place at the Algonquin Roundtable.

"Her graham cracker pie is the best." There's a sentence that's simplistic in both structure and truth. The truth is always simple. It's just the way things are. Trust me when I tell you her graham cracker pie was truly the best, hands down. And it, too, was very simple. It consisted of a homemade graham cracker crust which was finely crumbled and held together with melted butter. The pie shell was then packed with a rich, sugary vanilla pudding filling. This round batch of gooey goodness was then topped with a billowing mile-high mound of homemade meringue light enough to host a communal congregation of cherubs. The meringue was browned oh-so-slightly and speckled with little beads of vanilla. My aunt told me the vanilla was "little dots of heaven" and I had no reason to disbelieve her. Everything she created included a little dash of heaven.

Aunt Ruth's kitchen was an odd vortex, a window into another realm. It was a tiny room, so small you had to look at it twice to make sure you saw it. But whatever she conjured up in that small space was large enough to nourish a Kingdom and its surrounding territories…and, honestly, it often did. Her sugar cookies danced like the Rockettes on your tongue. Each and every one tasted of sheer synchronized perfection. Her chicken pot pie was so astonishingly good that, after years without it, I finally broke down and asked her to send me the recipe. She was tickled pink that I asked and promptly popped it out in the mail. When I opened the envelope I discovered it neatly written on a white index card that boasted a heading across the top: "From the Kitchen of Aunt Ruth." That was so her.

Things had to be done a certain way, the right way, and everything with a little flourish.

My favorite culinary nirvana that emitted from Aunt Ruth's kitchen (other than her graham cracker pie, of course, which was so good it deserved its own "best of" list on which it was the only entry) was a delectable little morsel she simply called "brown noodles." What's that, you ask? Egg noodles cooked in beef broth. That's it. Seriously, that's all there was to it. Just egg noodles and broth. But you know what? Only she could make it right. My grandmother made them for me once and it just wasn't the same. I don't know HOW one can screw up cooking egg noodles in beef broth but it happened. My grandmother cooked it and it was "meh." My aunt cooked it and my tummy petitioned to have a national holiday named in her honor. She had a knack, a special touch perhaps, that defies description.

Again, Aunt Ruth always wanted things to be done in a very specific way. She was always striving to make something lovely even more so. And not just in the kitchen. No, her abilities expanded well beyond the boundaries of the kitchen. While a lone flower can enhance a vase on a table just imagine what a handful of carefully arranged flowers would do! If you gave her a few strands of hay, some sticks and a bucket she would walk away with a beautiful bouquet while anyone else would just have a mound of mangy mulch. A new pair of shoes can accent an outfit but toss in a purse and matching earrings and you've got a fashion statement! The lady had style. She had a certain look about her and it spread to anything and everything she enhanced along her way. She could have marked her handiwork by posting a sign reading "RUTH WAS HERE" but it wasn't necessary. You just knew.

If my aunt and uncle's home was a living, breathing entity, then the kitchen was the heart. Its pulse could be felt, sensed, in every nook and cranny of the house. There's a seemingly endless stream of photos of family meals. Countless celebrations recounted and collected via Kodak. The flipping of photos gives an astonishing timeline of fashion, family and mashed potato presentation through the decades. While the faces age and styles change, the look of satisfied happiness does not. And, at the center of it all, was the flawless handiwork of my Aunt Ruth.

Everything had to be done just so. Nothing could or would be discarded or dismissed. Just like her sister, everything was useful. And everything had to look a certain way. From table presentation to personal appearance to the placement of refrigerator magnets. There was no escaping it. She herself often admitted her own concern over what others—strangers included—thought about, well, everything that she did, cooked, cleaned or wore. But, with her distinctive style, the only thing anyone could honestly think was, "Wow! That' the best!"

Aunt Ruth was my partner in crime as I was growing up. She would help me sneak surprise holiday gifts for my mom into the house right under Mom's nose. Mom was often mystified how her 13-year-old son was able to attain items only available from a store 20 miles away. Clearly, I was already flexing my telekinetic muscles. Aunt Ruth would encourage me to try new selections on a menu. She planted the seeds of my odd love of obnoxiously loud shirts. She encouraged my art, my writing, my theater work in high school and college and, eventually, my own mediumship. After seeing me give a mediumship group demonstration for the first time, she said, "You were born to do that, you know? You were just born to do that." Yup, she got me. I could be myself around her, eccentric faults and all, and never be questioned. She would encourage me to push the envelope in order to pursue my anything-but-normal dreams. Like a home away from home, she was my Mom away from Mom.

My aunt and uncle's home was the first family home I entered when I was adopted. I was in their living room before the one I would be sharing with my (NEW & IMPROVED!) Mom and Dad. Hers was the second phone number I ever memorized.

Some of my fondest memories growing up were when I was allowed to spend a few days with Aunt Ruth and Uncle Bill without my mother or grandparents! Oh, the juvenile nirvana! My stays there always had a particular formula: a visit to Hill's Department Store and Ace Hardware because they had the best toy departments in town. Mom would give me a spending allowance of $3 for these mad shopping binges. Yes, kiddies, you could get some pretty cool stuff for three bucks back in the pre-Amazon days. This venture would be followed by lunch at either a burger joint or pizza place. This was long before ordering mass produced chemically enhanced food through a flashing marquee from the coziness of your SUV.

Then we'd go home where we would play whatever game I bought. She would then make dinner while I read a comic book or watched cartoon animals parade across the TV screen (clearly a precursor to what was lurking down the road for me). My uncle, a local truck driver, often worked late. Sometimes he'd have dinner with us, sometimes not. When he'd come home after I had gone to bed, he'd make a point to come into the room I had commandeered, sit on the bed and talk with me about my day, his day and everything in between. I'd enthusiastically gush over all we'd done that day and he was seemingly hanging on my every blabbering word. He, too, always made me feel not just welcome, but one of his own family.

What seemed like such mundane things then now have such great significance. Funny how that happens, huh?

I always loved watching my aunt and uncle together. My parents divorced when I was very young so I didn't have the experience of growing up in a two-parent household. Although I grew up in my grandparent's home and saw them together every day, it just wasn't the same. Aunt Ruth and Uncle Bill were of my mom's generation so they gave me clearer idea of just how Team Parent worked. My mother had to pull double duty as both mom and dad so I found my aunt and uncle quite intriguing. I often ogled them as if they were my own little science experiment or a set of sea monkeys I could order from an ad in a comic book. They coordinated and worked together as a team with some duties overlapping and others being separate. The raising of the children was, of course, a team effort, as was care of the home. Uncle Bill handled the mind-numbing task of mowing the world's biggest backyard from my adolescent point of view (I swear it was so big it could have had its own representative in the senate!). While he took great care in keeping a neatly trimmed yard, Aunt Ruth made a point to doll up the interior. The beauty of the home they shared was only enhanced by the same grace and love they had for one another. Sure, they squabbled like any couple, but their love was always evident no matter what the situation. She often referred to him as her sweetheart both before and after his death. She had each and every love letter my uncle had written to her while stationed overseas during WWII. Each one ended longingly with, "PS I Love You." Even at 95 she would blush like a lovelorn teenager when talking about him.

Uncle Bill left us in 1985. Twenty-nine years later I watched his wife draw her last breath in order to rejoin the sweetheart she'd had since she was 15. A love for the ages if there ever was one.

It was fitting that she left us within the cozy confines of the home she established and ran with such love. It is where she wanted to be and, therefore, we did, too. She was surrounded by those she loved—her son & daughter-in-law, her baby sister, one of her six granddaughters & her husband, and an uncharacteristically quiet nephew donning an Hawaiian shirt that could be heard across the street. She was always one to think of others. She would place the comfort and wants of another ahead of her own. That's why it is particularly fitting that her final act of coherence was to tell each of us, "I love you." Once again, she did it her own way. The best way.

Her funeral service was held two days before Christmas in the church she loved nearly as much as her own home. Again, her command of doing things "just so" was fully evident. The sanctuary was decked out in full Christmas Pageantry. The serenity and beauty literally defied description. Rows of red and white poinsettia's lined the alter. Every single petal was perfectly poised and positioned. The lights twinkled in a silent chorus from upon high. Sunshine glistened brightly through the stain glass windows illuminating the church interior as well as its inhabitants. Everyone was bathed in 61 degree sunlight. Yes, 61 degrees in late December. Unheard of in West Virginia. Leave it to my aunt to arrange the best weather! The service and surroundings were, as she often said, "a picture... it's just a picture."

Admittedly, I did not focus on the service itself but, instead, the energies joining us. I know she was there — I cannot tell you how often the guest of honor will give me a review of their own funeral — so I did my best to "listen." It was, of course, difficult. It's hard to take a clinical approach to a passing when you have such an emotional investment. At one point, I thought, assumedly to myself, "I wonder what it's like for her right now..."

As clear as a bell, I heard Aunt Ruth's all too familiar voice. In a tone of absolute awe, she simply said, "It's a rainbow!" I was so stunned at the clarity that I believe I actually gasped. And then I smiled. Leave it to her to give the best answer.

So, like her graham cracker pie, her attire & attitude, her outlook & outreach, my Aunt Ruth is, and shall always be, the best.

"INTENTION INTERVENTION"

"Be your own face value, the living embodiment of your word. Your actions are not merely a reflection of your intentions—they ARE part of you, no different than a limb or muscle. Every move, every reaction, every intention speaks volumes. Do your part to ensure that what you are saying is indeed what you want heard."

The Collective

I DON'T MAKE MANY DEMANDS IN MY LIFE. I just have a small handful of requirements in order to make various experiences more enjoyable, tolerable. Never serve me a sandwich with mayonnaise on or near it. Never put lemon in my tea for any reason because no good will come of it. Never, under any circumstance, sing along with the radio if you're in my home or car. And, finally, just leave me the hell alone when I'm traveling. Don't talk to me, approach me or, if possible, even exhale in my direction. I have a particularly deep intolerance of chatty taxi drivers. Drive, don't speak, and we'll get along famously. I have no idea why I'm this way. I'm completely fine with Joe Shmoe Stranger striking up a conversation with me if I'm standing in line at my local post office. But if I'm in an airport just get away from me as if I haven't bathed in a fortnight.

My Guides are always nudging me to get out of my routine, to shake things up a bit. Nudge, in this case, is an all-too-polite euphemism for treating me like their own personal Whack-A-Mole. So, against my better judgment and instinct, I gave their advice a shot when a moment of so-called opportunity presented itself.

I was dragging my sleepy self onto the commuter tram in the Pittsburgh Airport after enduring a redeye flight from LA last December. The sparse pedestrian population in the terminal told me that my flight was probably one of the first to come in that morning. I made my way to the tram quickly and quietly with absolutely no interaction. When I boarded I was most pleased to see that there was only one other person on the train. There's nothing like open space after being stuffed in an overly populated flying sardine can for several hours. My fellow traveler looked up at me from her newspaper as I stepped on the train. She simply said, "Good morning."

I responded in kind. Then, after a moment, I thought I'd push that envelope Robert & Crew are constantly throwing up at me. So I added, "Merry Christmas."

Boy, was that a mistake. She whipped her head up from her newspaper as her eyes widened. "I don't celebrate Christmas!" she hissed.

Without missing a beat I replied, "And Christmas is the better for it."

She turned her self-righteous nose back into her periodical as I rolled my eyes. Bonding ceased at that very instant.

So what was the point of this delightful experience with this human Care Bear? Well, for one thing, it's given me a great story. But it is also a damn fine lesson in the simple power of intent.

OK, so she doesn't celebrate Christmas. Big fat hairy deal. No one will ever accuse me of being Father Christmas. Scrooge's philosophy of the holiday being a poor excuse to pick a man's pocket every twenty-fifth day of December resonates deeply within me. However, I do understand the sincerity of passing along to another the simple, heartfelt wish for a Merry Christmas. I have Jewish friends who wish me a Happy Hanukah every year. I'm not Jewish—my covered dish encased Methodist upbringing proves that—but I am quite happy to receive their sincere wish. I can pass a Merry Christmas on to them and they, too, are good with it. Why? Because it's the intent, the sincerity, that rings true.

I understand that our opinions and beliefs are sacred to each of us. But why does one feel compelled to throw them in someone else's face in the most inopportune times? Why attempt to fill the big scheme of things with something so selfishly and insignificantly small? The woman just doesn't celebrate Christmas. Fine. But what's the harm of replying with a simple 'thank you' instead of an impassioned stance atop a portable soapbox? How can a simple seasonal salutation be regarded as offensive? What's next, people? Saying 'hi' to someone to only have them pummel you as they scream how they only accept 'hello' as an appropriate greeting?

Pick your battles, plan your platforms, and stop sweating the small stuff. We've taken ourselves far too seriously. We keep our heads buried in our own backyard and cringe at the idea of the different perspective of another. Think before you speak, before you act and react. Your intent will go farther than you may realize.

"Words may seem like feathers, virtually weightless as they blow along your way. But, when accumulated, the feathers can soar to the heavens… or they can blow apart and plummet. Where do your words and intent go? That, dear child, is up to you."

The One Who Soars with Eagles

"Grief Relief"

GRIEF IS AN ODD LITTLE THING, ISN'T IT? It continually changes and morphs. It is something very personal with each variation stamped with a unique moniker. Everyone handles it differently. I once had a neighbor who hit on women at the funeral of his wife of nearly 40 years. I know a woman who lost her husband, the love of her life, over 20 years ago and she still grieves to this day as if it just happened. I know of another who immediately closes the emotional door on anyone who passes away the instant the last breath is drawn. "I don't dwell on the past," he says. I know yet another who lost her husband nearly 30 years ago yet she visits his grave several times a week. Yes, grief is as diverse as the individuals it affects.

My Uncle Bill had a particularly putrid loathing of cemeteries. A highly practical man, his disdain stemmed from frank, lucid logic. "I can go into my backyard, stare at the ground and have the same memories of a person as I would if I drove to where they're buried. Why make the drive?" He then looked at me and said, "If you ever visit my grave I'm going to come back down here and kick your butt!"

<gulp> Yes, sir.

I attended his funeral, of course. The man was like a father to me. One year later I revisited his grave for the first time since his interment. As I stood there, staring at the grass now blanketing what he used to walk around in, I flashed back to that conversation. And, as is my custom in most situations, I began to laugh. It started as a chortle and climaxed into a glass shattering guffaw. In fact, I laughed so hard that I had to lean on his headstone in order to keep from falling over. I'm sure I was quite the spectacle for any nearby slack-jawed mourners. Upon regaining composure, or in my case the next best thing to being there, I said aloud, "OK, Uncle Bill, you win! I'm gone!" More than 20 years passed before I returned to his gravesite. Same grass, same stone, same memories, same love. Yup. We're good.

So, yeah, each of us handles it differently. While some internalize it, I tend to wear it on my sleeves like matching cufflinks. I wasn't like that in my youth, or even semi-youth. But when I finally accepted my mediumship, and the gates opened wide, EVERYTHING changed.

At this very moment my friend, Suzie, is gloating and laughing her head off. Shut up, you big, stupid dumb-dumb face. ♥

According to Elisabeth Kübler-Ross, the noted psychiatrist, there are five stages of grief: Denial, Anger, Bargaining, Depression and finally Acceptance. Each of us checks off that list at our own pace. Some fast, some slow and some just come to a screeching halt somewhere in between. I believe many individuals fear that achieving acceptance means you're over the loss and you've forgotten your loved one. Nope. Not even close. I believe acceptance is simply the clinical term for that blessed moment when the sorrow moves to the back seat and the fond, loving memories call shotgun and move to the forefront.

I'm often asked if my being a medium makes me numb to grief and loss. I answer that with a resounding, "Oh, HELL no!" If anything, I think it makes me even more sensitive to it. Sure, on a spiritual level, I have a different perception of death. But the physical emptiness is strong and dominant. I cannot take a clinical approach to loss. I do my best to remain detached while giving a reading but I don't always succeed. The all-too-human emotions are sometimes so strong that it will bowl me over. I've been known to shed tears alongside the sitter from time to time. But I do not regret it one iota. Emotions are part of what makes us human. And, whether you like it or not, we're all human this time around. Do not try to raise yourself above it because it won't do you one bit of good. Face it down. Stand with it. Embrace it. Unlike a priest offering marital advice, I am speaking to you from first-hand experience. There are no assumptions here, kiddies. It's all far too real.

I have always tried to work through my personal losses to the best of my stumbling abilities. And, like anyone, I don't always succeed. The most severe example of this was the sudden death of my dear friend, Leigh, in 2007.

Gloating over our complete obliteration of one of many poor, unsuspecting dinners.

Appropriately, I began penning this on her 8th Angel Day and wrapped it up on the eighth anniversary of my receiving the news of her death. Each year without her still rattles through me with a haunting echo. She was my left arm. We were joined at the hip, thinking and reacting as one at times. The sun and moon often ran complete cycles during our marathon conversations. We once spent a good four hours sitting on the balcony of a hotel in San Diego doing nothing but conversing as if we were on police radios. It began, innocently enough, when a police officer on the sidewalk far below was apprehending a fleeing person of interest. The officer, upon tackling the lad to the sandy floor, radioed for some assistance. So we decided to offer our half of the unheard conversation. This improvisation lead us to creating approximately 8 or 9 different characters, all with distinctly diverse voices, evolving into a barrage of subplots and subtexts that would leave the bard himself utterly speechless. We were in tears. Never in our lives had we (or anyone else for that matter) been so brilliantly funny. Amaretto can do that, you know?

For the most part I have worked through her passing. But, as usual, I hopscotch to my own beat. I never work on my cartooning work in sequence. I just go where my whims take me so why should my handling of grief be any different? Denial was pretty quick. I just ripped off that band aid with a fast and furious jerk. There wasn't much time spent within the bargaining column. Whenever anyone dies my first response is, "And yet we still have Carrot Top?" I'm willing to trade him in on anyone. "Bring my hamster back and you can have Carrot Top!" I'll exclaim, but that's another story for another time. I know I've accepted that she's gone. Well, physically, anyway. As many of you know she does tend to pop up from time to time, thankfully.

If you've attended any of my group readings I always have a chair reserved on the front row just for her. She always gives me a sign at some point during the evening that she really is there, with one lone exception. Due to the space and configuration of the room I placed her chair in the back row instead of in the front. She made it perfectly clear to me that this was NOT acceptable by giving me absolutely no hint of any kind that she was in attendance. So, to this day, her chair is always in the very front no matter what. Yeah, I'm whipped.

It is eight years later, and I am still angry about it. Yes, depression is a small zit protruding on the forehead of anger. I'm the first to admit that. But it is anger that, like Leigh herself, takes a position in the front row.

Why? Well, I'll tell you…

I have been very blessed to be a part of an amazing process. I have been honored time and time again to help connect those in Spirit to those here in the physical. It really is a gift. The gift isn't so much being able to do this work as much as it is being fortunate enough to be a part of it and to witness it firsthand. I do not do it myself. Nope. I'm just the middleman, the bridge. I don't lay claim to being some kind of oracle or anything equally outlandish. I am simply where I need to be and doing what I need to do. End of story. I have experienced miraculous reunions between parents and children, brothers and sisters, dear friends from both long ago and recent days, even pet owners and their "fur babies." Time and time again I am mystified by the whole process. I have been given the chance to help so many individuals throughout my years of service with Spirit. Most of these individuals are complete strangers to me. Some return for more sessions while others go on with their lives, sharing their healing with those who will listen. It's all just so breathtaking.

My anger stems from a very selfish place: I have helped so many strangers but why couldn't I help someone who was so close to me? Why wasn't I given a heads up so I could prevent it from happening? WHY? I get to tell someone to watch out for an upcoming auto repair. I've been given information on the much needed repaving of their driveway. But I am NOT able to save a life of someone I truly love, a piece of my very own heart? Sure, I know what you're saying… "It was meant to be." Do you really think that makes it any better? Nope, it doesn't. I am perfectly aware I have been having a major temper tantrum over the whole thing. I feel like I want to take my mediumship ball and just go home.

So, as you can see, I grieve just as anyone else. There's no Get Out of Jail Free card for me.

Don't get me wrong. I'm still working and I will until I draw my last line or breath, whichever comes first. But every now and again the anger barges through and that's when things get bad. How bad, you ask? I had two heart attacks in 2006. They were nearly 5 weeks apart. There was nothing on TV so I thought, "Hey, let's try something new!" FYI: NOT a great way to kill some time. Just sayin'.

In the beginning I followed my cardiologist's words as if they had come down from upon high. I was walking the walk and talking the talk. And let me tell you Leigh was holding me accountable on everything. She demanded I give her my doctor's contact information, a list of all of my meds, the diet I was following, you name it. It's a wonder she didn't have a chip imbedded in my skull. (Note to self: inspect your scalp for any unusual scars in the bathroom mirror later tonight) She was my task master and I towed the line, no questions asked. She took no prisoners while she was here and that trait hasn't changed on the other side. She always shot from the hip, ricochets be damned.

Then, one horrible morning, she was gone. And I have to say I just stopped caring at that point. I didn't give a damn about much of anything. Everything seemed pretty pointless for the most part. It wasn't like a light being turned off. It was more like *I* turned the light off myself. I didn't care to see what was around me. And I just stayed there… Not good, Charlie, not good.

This year is different, however. It feels different. Leigh always called me on my crap. I couldn't get away with anything with her—and I did the same with her. She was direct. There's no doubt about that. She once gave me what I consider to be the greatest compliment I have ever received. Out of the blue she called me and said she HAD to see me that weekend. She was flying from her home in Chicago just to see me so I was ordered to drop everything and prepare for her arrival. Fortunately, I never had anything to drop so it was all pretty effortless. Over dinner I asked, "Why the urgency to visit?"

She looked at me over her wine glass and said simply, "I needed to be with the one person who knows my bullshit is nothing but bullshit."

It doesn't get any better than that in my book.

Well, you know what? I had forgotten that MY bullshit is exactly that, too. Bullshit. But she wasn't here to call me on it. Or so I thought. She found little subtle avalanches that would get my attention throughout today's anniversary. I always welcome these signs. It always amuses and amazes me how they can find a way to get through to us. I rarely get direct messages from my loved ones, however. They almost always rely on signs and/or reaching out to me through what I term as a "disinterested third party." I don't trust myself to get out of the way when it comes to personal communication. I have a vivid imagination—it is my livelihood after all!—so I just leave it to someone else.

But sometimes, when it is needed, they kick down the door and just yell at me. Today was one of those days. I was picking up a few items from the local market when I found myself being lured by the seductive catcalls of the bakery. Donuts and I have had a long-lasting affair for decades. As my eyes grazed over the glass display case I heard an all-too-familiar voice scream in my head, "CHANGE IT, DON'T BLAME IT!"

I spun around and, of course, she wasn't there. (But, of course, she was.) She called me on it one more time.

So, yeah, it's time to change for good, literally and figuratively. I'm going to change the anger, the reasons, the emptiness. It won't happen overnight and I'm good with that. But it does have to change. Blaming gets us nowhere. I was angry and rightfully so. However, it was not right STAYING that way. It's a discredit to her memory, her soul, and it is incredibly disrespectful to me. If you don't allow someone to disrespect you then how on earth can you allow yourself to do it? Do as I say, not as I do is NOT a way to live…it's an excuse. You can't live in the anger…you have to wade through it and come out on the other side in order to accept THEY are on their other side.

But, God, what a blessing knowing they break through connecting their never ceasing hearts with ours so we all truly beat as one.

You know what? As I finished writing this piece the song "Friend Like Me" from Aladdin started playing. What an ideal seal of her "it's all about me" approval! And she's right, you know? I never have had a friend like her but I know she will always be with me. 10-4, Leigh… I love you, too.

"One Mother of a Day for Two"

WHICH CAME FIRST? The chicken or the egg? The age-old quandary. Either point can be argued. There's no doubt about that. And, honestly, I don't believe either answer will ever fully win out over the other. Therefore I'd like to toss my own theory in the philosophical ring o' fire: no matter which one it was I'm willing to bet that a mother was behind it. Mom's always there, on some level, within each of us. So why should a chicken or an egg be any different? All signs point to mom, mother, mommie dearest, maw, mumsy… call her what you like but we all know who we're talking about, don't we?

As Mother's Day leaps from the calendar once more, I can't help but mull over my own mother and her own attempts at steering a nearly rudderless boat through a multitude of choppy seas. Being the mother of an anti-social nerd with a mindset bordering on the unexplainable would have driven anyone weaker to drink. Honestly, I don't know how Mom got through it. She's a gutsy broad who loves a challenge and, boy oh boy, did she get one in me. She herself has told me that, as a child, she wasn't a fan of cartoons. Then her only child becomes a cartoonist. Who says God doesn't have the wackiest sense of humor EVER? But she pulled it off with a minimum of gray hairs. If she had any nervous breakdowns she had the decency to have them quietly and without fanfare. I once asked her how she managed to not kill me during my teenage years of angst and agony. She simply replied dryly, "Fear of prison." A wise woman. As the saying goes, "Patience is what you learn when there are too many witnesses."

Upon reflection that often resembles a fun house mirror, I have chosen a couple of my mom's parenting decisions that I rate as her best and truly wisest. Two moments, plucked from far too many to list, that truly stand out to me as life altering, as well as affecting, moments that helped make me who I am today (Now you know who to blame).

The family—meaning Mom, myself and my grandfather—vacationed in Virginia Beach, Virginia in the summer of 1975. This was our first big trip since the passing of my grandmother just over a year and a half earlier. Needless to say it was a bit odd for all of us. We were still adjusting to the absence of one of our immediate own. The film JAWS was released while we were in Virginia Beach. I begged, pleaded and groveled before my mother in order to let me go see this movie! I all but bribed her but, since I only got a $2.00 allowance every two weeks, I didn't have a lot of leeway. "If you let me go see this movie now," I'd say, "I'll give you a dollar and then another dollar when it's over!" And that's how the Wolf of Wall Street was born. Despite throwing myself on the mercy of the court, Mom would have no part of it. "We'll see it when we get home," she ruled. Needless to say, I was livid. She was SO MEAN! She never let me do ANYTHING fun! Waaa Waaa and Waaa some more. I pouted, brooded and sulked like a paparazzi that just ran out of film. I'm sure my mother, on the other hand, simply enjoyed the silence. So, as ordered from the Powers Upon High, I waited until we returned home to see the movie that everyone, but me, was talking about.

Oh, Sweet Mother of God. Best decision EVER. In all of history, my mother's verdict to not let me see JAWS in Virginia Beach ranks right up there with the decision of the first life form to crawl out of the primal ooze in order to walk upon dry land and the universal choice to end disco. If I had gone to see it while AT the beach, I would have NEVER gone NEAR the water again let alone actually IN it. I probably would have stayed on the boardwalk with my grandfather. Who am I kidding? I would have just moved into the backseat of Mom's Dodge Dart and waited until we went home.

Well played, Mom. Well played indeed.

You must be wondering how she could top that flawless parental veto. "It can't be done!" you exclaim. "Oh, yes it can," I coo. And here it is…

My mother was always, from Day One, completely open with me about my adoption. I do not know of a time when I did not know I was adopted. She has told me that she talked to me about it when I was too young to even comprehend what she was saying (yet before my teenage years when I just tuned out everything she said). This simple act of honesty truly made THE biggest difference in my life. This seemingly simple act encompassed my past, my present and my future.

I doubt if I can fully explain the significance of this to someone who is not an adoptee. Little things like recognizing that you have grandma's eyes to knowing the exact time of your own birth, are just run-of-the-mill snippets of your life that are rarely given a second thought. I was 33 years of age before I found out the time of my birth. I had always been told it was "around five in the morning." At 33 I discovered it was 4:42am. Big deal, right? For me it was. I stayed up until 4:42am when my 34th birthday—the first after finding my birth family—rolled around. And I've met many adoptees who have done the exact same thing.

I was even denied the classic parental lament, "I was in labor for 18 hours with you, ya know!" The best my mom could offer up was, "I got writer's cramp filling out all of those adoption forms, ya know!" It just doesn't have the same effect. Mom easily and effortlessly passed on what little information she had regarding my biological parents. Sadly, the bulk of what she was told, other than the name of my birthmother, was nothing but a tapestry of intentional lies and bullshit. To the state of West Virginia, I was not a human being. I was a product that needed to be moved off the shelf. It's a wonder that I didn't have AS SEEN ON TV stamped on my forehead. Mom gave me all of the paperwork that she had regarding my adoption. This was the first time I saw my birthmother's signature. Again, something that so many would take for granted. I remember running my finger over it, tracing the line of her pen, thinking this was my first connection with the woman who actually gave birth to me. She had, at one time, touched this piece of paper I now held in my own hands. Shivers went through me. It was finally real.

Less than two months after my 33rd birthday, I spoke to my birthmother for the very first time. Two weeks after that came the first face-to-face meeting and the first barrage of hugs, tears and, of course, laughs. Later that year, my mom hosted a dinner in the home I grew up in for the woman whose home I never knew. Mom played hostess—a roll she has always cherished—to a gaggle of my blood: my birthmother, three of my four siblings from her side, and four of my nieces and nephews. An undertaking that would be both physically and emotionally daunting for your average bear, but not my mom. For her it was just a celebration of a life long journey for, frankly, both of us.

I will tell you this, however… having Dueling Mothers at the dinner table is a bit spooky. I was half expecting to hear "Why aren't you a doctor?" and "Why aren't you married yet?" in stereo.

What stood out for me—and still does to this day—is a very small, nearly undetectable moment that I almost didn't witness. The brood was leaving and saying their goodbyes. The siblings were all outside wrangling kids and insulting one another, as good siblings do. I was standing on the porch, just outside the front storm door. The Mom's were on the other side of the door, in the living room. I glanced over my shoulder, looking at them through the mesh screen. My birthmother, Joyce, thanked mom for a lovely meal and, of course, my mother thanked her for coming. They hugged and Joyce softly said through tears, "Thank you for taking care of my boy."

My mom, in a choked voice, replied, "Thank you for having him. I don't know what I would have done without him."

Not a dry eye in the house…or on the porch, either.

As a medium, I am privy to some pretty amazing things. I have witnessed countless reunions and connections. I have seen love and humility come together in emotional bursts of light that defy description. But what I saw, and heard, that day truly ranks as the single most beautiful experience of my life. At the time, of course, I had no idea it was only a precursor to what I would observe along my life path as a medium. I often reflect back on that exchange during my own readings. My memory helps ground me. It helps me better understand what is taking place between the sitter and their non-physical visitor.

Spirit always utilizes the card file of memories in my head in order to help me better understand their messages, their intent and, of course, their never-ending love. And, I gotta tell ya, I love it when they bring that particular memory back up to bob around on the surface.

Even my mother's decision to not let me see JAWS has its own place in the roots of my spiritual work. Spirit gives me what the sitter can handle and nothing more. Spirit passes along information and insight intended for the best of all parties involved. In the big scheme of things my mom was doing the same thing.

I guess you can say Spirit is just one big mother. Wait. That sounded better in my head...

I am where, and who, I am today because of the generosity and love of two different women (who eerily look alike, but that's beside the point). One was brave enough to give me, what she felt, was a chance at a better life than she could provide. The other was strong enough to open her heart to, literally, the unknown, in order to enrich both of our lives. I, on the other hand, just sat there like a lump and bobbed through the waves.

I have two mothers. One is here, the other is in spirit. But, without a shadow of a doubt, both reside within me, my actions & thoughts and, most significantly, my heart. Because, as with the chicken & the egg, "Mom" is always a part of me.

"The Blue Set Me Free"

"I ask that you look within yourself for the strength and focus you are seeking. It is said that the best way to hide something is within plain view. I assure you this is the case with you. It is right there before your eyes, within your heart."

Robert

WE OFTEN FOCUS ON ALL OF THE HUGE MONSTROSITIES OF LIFE but, when push comes to shove, we always come back to the things we think should be insignificant. Have you noticed that thinking generally leads to trouble? We can fail to remember some remarkable things but find ourselves focusing on that playmate unseen since the second grade. Why is that? I think that on some subterranean level we know that the big things are, indeed, made up of all those small things. When I hear from a Spirit I find that their 'regrets', for lack of a better word, are not those of overwhelming tsunamis. I have yet to have someone relate to me something along the lines of, "I wish I had ignored more people" or "I sure wish I had six cars instead of the four" or even "I so wish I had spent even more time at the office and less time with my family." What I am told is that they wish they had truly stopped and smelled the roses along the way or that they had spent more time being aware of those around them. Sounds like something out of Jacob Marley's mouth, doesn't it? Let me tell you there's a lot of truth within the quill of Charles Dickens. I have been told, on more than one occasion, how they wish they had taken the time to simply smile and greet a total stranger while passing on the street.

Once I hit the infamous "Big-Four-Oh" I have made a point, each year, to take a trip to mark my birthday. I've never been one to acknowledge my birthday in the past. As a child I would literally run and hide in a closet while the party-goers caterwauled an ear-splitting rendition of "Happy Birthday to You". It didn't matter if it was my birthday or someone else's. The song would get my feet moving and my heart pumping. Is it because I'm an adoptee and my birthday somehow reminds my subconscious of the ultimate personal rejection? Or is it because I'm just plain weird? I'm sure the therapists reading this are just salivating over the prospect of writing a thesis on me and my phobias.

I had decided to celebrate my 45th in The Emerald City of Seattle for a few days stretching over the day my peephole was opened, as Mr. Vonnegut would say. However, my plans were sidetracked by a sudden and unplanned illness so I had to postpone my flight. I was infuriated at the prospect of being stuck at home for my birthday. After all, this was the obviously larger-but-never-gets-the-same-press "Damn-Big-Four-Five". With notoriety like that under my belt I had no intention of celebrating at the local IHOP. I don't have anything against IHOP. It's just this isn't the venue to write about my obsessive, bordering on the perverse, love of Boysenberry Syrup.

I boarded a train bound for Santa Barbara and, from there, planned on renting a car for a two-and-a-half hour tool up the highway to Morro Bay. I'd never been there so, what the heck? Different scenery, different attitude, and all that hype. But there was a method to my seemingly aloof madness. All the best divine madness has a basis; an epicenter. Just 30 minutes further north from the coastal paradise of Morro Bay is the quiet little town of Cambria. And it was there, not Morro Bay, that I had marked the true X on my map.

Cambria was where she had lived. Her turf. Sherlock Holmes referred to Irene Adler as The Woman. A title that was given by Mr. Holmes out of intellectual respect for Miss Adler as well as personal emotional heartbreak. My Irene Adler went by the name of Michelle. Yes, her. The woman. The nightmare. The train wreck in stilettos. I had one last bit of business with her and the time for the stockholders meeting had arrived. I dared tell no one what I was doing because I knew I would get a series of lectures accented with an avalanche of rolling eyes. This was for me and, I assume, for her as well. OK. Who am I trying to kid? It was all about me. By the way, if anyone would appreciate this narcissistic streak it would have been Michelle.

The Amtrak ride to Santa Barbara was uneventful which was fine by me. The sprawling Pacific stalked me on my left most of the way up only to be obliterated from time to time by various islands of billboards and warehouses embellished in graffiti. I dozed, as is my custom, so my visual memories of the ride were almost a panoramic Morse code of images and sounds. After retrieving my suitcase—I was the only passenger who checked luggage (a tribute to my own divine laziness)—I embarked on the quarter-mile stroll to the car rental agency. I take great pride in my ability to correctly select the car I will be given nearly every-single-time. My slate blue eyes scanned the lot and fixated on a small red sedan off to the left. "That's it," I thought to myself. And I smiled smugly knowing that "Super Psychic" had done it once again.

I was knocked down a few pegs within seconds of entering the sparsely furnished lobby of the rental agency. The clerk behind the counter, who couldn't possibly try harder if his life depended on it, slammed a lone key attached to a plastic tag onto the counter encased in genuine fake paneling. I saw the word WHITE staring up at me from within the cozy rectangular key chain. The Universe: 1. Psychic Boy: El Zippo. Upon further examination I discovered that I would be, for the next three days anyway, the proud legal guardian of a Chevrolet Cobalt. Cobalt: as in the color. Leave it to me to get my hands on a white car named after a shade of blue. It's sad that I find little snippets of information like that even remotely interesting or amusing. Just take my word for it when I tell you that it is a vital sliver of this tale.

I entered the city limits of Cambria just after eleven on the morning of my 45th birthday. After some thought I've decided that there's no better time to seek a rebirth than on your own birthday. The best thing about that idea is that I won't have to remember a different date in order to celebrate. Enlightenment and ease make great bedfellows. This is the same logic used when a man insists his upcoming wedding be on Valentine's Day: the chances of forgetting are virtually nil. Laziness cleverly described as romance. You've got to love that logic.

I was actually somewhat stunned to find that Cambria is quite a rural community. From the way Michelle had described it I was expecting anything but what I found. Finding that this upper crust snob was actually living within walking distance of cows was nothing short of astonishing. If she were still alive I would have called and heckled her. Well, actually, I'm pretty cheap. I would have just sent a post card.

With directions gripped firmly in one hand and the steering wheel of my misnamed white rental car in the other I drove straight to her former home. I have no idea why I needed to see this house. I felt the overwhelming urge to see some physical representation of her brevity here on earth. I wanted to see, once and for all, the place she had spent so much time with me (via the telephone or computer). Is it possible to return to an unknown home? I couldn't figure out why but, for one of the few times in my life, I really didn't care about the 'why' of it all. 'Why' suddenly became replaced with 'Why Not'. What a kick. Rebirth brings on change whether it is big or small. Come to think of it there is no such thing as a 'small' change. Change takes courage, desire and determination (none of which deserves any form of mockery). Any type of change is definitely anything but small. Remember, my friends, 'small' is never to be confused with 'insignificant'.

I found the home with ease. This is, of course, quite a surprise, since I get lost more frequently than an amnesiac. Even with directions I can still get lost. I don't know whether to laugh or cry, honestly. So I just do both. It keeps people talking… I parked the white Cobalt across the street, slowly stepped out of the car, then just stood there and stared. I began to slowly shake my head in disbelief as a half-laugh fell from my throat. The first thing that caught my eye was the front door of the house.

The cobalt blue front door.

I spent, at best, ten minutes there. I figured I should leave so the neighbors wouldn't call the police thinking I was casing the joint for a future burglary. I tried to imagine Michelle pulling into her driveway and sitting on her deck like any normal person. But I suspect that there were more fireworks going on in that house than on the Mall in DC on the Fourth of July. Normalcy, in her home, as in her life, was probably quite the rarity. It was difficult to view a home that I was, at one time, planning to share with the woman I loved. If things had worked out—if she had actually been the person she pretended to be with me—that would have been where I would be parking my car. I would have been sitting with her on that unspectacular deck under the stars. My life—our lives—would have been completely different. Yes, when I first heard of this home in 1997, I fully intended to be standing before it but not as I am at this writing. I barely remember the person I thought I was going to be at that time and place. But he did, and on some level, still does exist. And the time had come for him and me to meet once more and then, for the last time, part company. There is no animosity between the two of us. Why would there be? But we do share the regret of what had been promised and knowing now, full well, that it would have never turned out that way.

I silently bid her farewell, returned to my temporary car, and left. I left the memories and the realities of her waded in a ball dropped on her former doorstep. I left her energy and her memory behind… I left the illusion of us behind… I left her behind. Or so I thought. It was barely twelve noon and the day had only just begun.

As I drove away with Michelle Estates diminishing in my rear view mirror I found myself muttering, "OK, now what?" (When will I ever learn?) Before I could give myself a chance to answer—yes I admittedly not only talk to myself but often consult myself on a great many topics—I made an abrupt left turn off the Cabrillo Highway and headed straight into downtown Cambria. Once again the classic 'why' had been replaced with the Perry Como Mellow 'why not'. I was pleasantly surprised to find that the bulk of downtown consists of antique stores or, as I like to call them, 'Expensive Flea Markets'. I pulled into a parking lot of one of these fine touristy establishments and waltzed inside. I was immediately enthralled with more useless junk than I could ever imagine. I was in nirvana. I wanted to own virtually every single item within my sight. It really would be pointless for me to win the lottery because I'd blow the bulk of my wealth on inane bobbles. Case in point: I spent nearly 30 minutes talking myself out of buying a walking stick that was made of a pool cue. The handle was an 8 ball. I have absolutely no use for that monstrosity but, ya know what? I almost bought it. This is a perfect example when 'why not' is not the best attitude!

Instead, my eye was caught by a piggy bank of all things. I was drawn to it as if it owned me. It stands eight inches in height and weighs nearly five pounds. What is this antiquity that screamed 'take me home with you' at the top of its imaginary lungs? Wimpy. Yes, Wimpy, of "Popeye" fame. As a small child my grandmother—Mamaw as all three of her grandchildren called her—dubbed me 'Wimpy' because of my cult-like devotion to the almighty hamburger. "I will gladly pay you Tuesday yadda-yadda-yadda…" The instant I saw the bank I just laughed. The same giggle one expects from a child or the Pillsbury Doughboy. After the morning's excursion into the memory of Michelle I needed a boost and Wimpy certainly provided just that. The instant I saw it I felt as if it was already mine. Of course, since the proprietor would probably not go along with my instinct, I felt it was best if I paid the $32.50 plus tax. In all honesty it was this purchase, and not my common sense, that prevented me from swaggering out twirling a pool cue cane in my chubby hand.

Wimpy called shotgun as I slid under the steering wheel. For a brief moment, as I snapped my seat belt, I thought that maybe Mamaw had her hand in my newly found treasure. I shook my head and laughed, as is my custom in most cases, and shrugged it off. Despite my working with Spirit I still have a hard time believing that they will take time out of their daily schedule and mess with us in the oddest of places, such as when we wander through an antique store. When will I learn? (My Guides have asked that very question countless times…)

So, off I went, with Wimpy at my side. I swear I fully intended to leave town at that point. But that thought burst into flames when I saw a sign with one word printed upon it; one word that could make me salivate in a Pavlovian response that only rivaled my love of mass produced cream-filled pastry. The word was "Cemetery". Without even a flash of hesitation I turned the car up the winding hillside road leading to the structured resting place of several unknown souls (well, to me anyway). Another why/why not moment.

If you even vaguely know me you know that I've always adored cemeteries. As a small child I would want to stop at every single one that we would pass in the car and, of course, cry if they would not do so. It goes without saying that I cried in the car a lot. I feel a history beneath my feet as I walk through the rows of stones bearing names, dates and messages. I find it nothing short of totally fascinating and, interestingly enough, calming. Calming to my body, my mind, my soul.

Congratulations, Charles. You've just become a psychiatrist's wet dream.

I parked the Chevy Cobalt beneath the spreading limbs of one of those tree things that nature-folk seem to go ga-ga over. Maple, oak, Norwegian moss dangler—I have no clue what kind it is. It was big and leafy; that about covers it. It's a good thing that Euell Gibbons isn't one of my guides. He would have torn a hole through the veil and bonked me over the head with a box of Grape Nuts for that.

As I got out of the car I was mesmerized at the beauty displayed before me. This was certainly a graveyard that was treated with great respect, love and honor. It's not one of those generic cookie-cutter corpse farms. You know the kind? The ones where all the head stones are flat plaques so the minimum wage 'landscaper', who usually boasts a monosyllabic surname, can easily roll over them on his John Deere while guzzling a brewsky wedged in his beer helmet. The tombstones in the Cambria Cemetery range from old and ornate to stylish and new. Flat, upright, carved statues, you name it. And the flowers! Oh, the beautiful flowers! And so many of the graves were decorated with statues, windmills, personal belongings… Each individual resting place was an extension of not only the person laid to rest there but of their loved ones as well. It was moving. A lot of care went into this sacred place and it showed. Of all the beauty sensed and demonstrated in this small cemetery the one item of note that blew me away was that even the unknown graves were not forgotten. If a simple rock marked the resting place of one known but to God it was embellished with some flowers. Someone was making a point to honor the memory of these individuals, even if we had no conscious memories of them. Some were marked with a simplistic verse: "Lost in name but not in spirit." Simply put: 'wow'.

I was immediately pulled, harshly, to a small headstone off to my left. I learned a long time ago to just go with the flow in times like this. It was the resting place of a woman by the name of Mae Harrison. Mae had lived well into her 83rd year on this side of the veil. Neither the name nor the dates meant anything to me. But the other inscription on the simple marker stopped me in my tracks. Mae was forever honored with the title "Loving Mother & Mamaw". Yes… Mamaw.

So, I was right. Mamaw had, indeed, directed me first to the metal Wimpy bank and now this cemetery, and then specifically to this grave just to let me know she was pulling the strings. What could I do but listen and watch? You know, I honestly believe I have spoken with Mamaw more now than when she was alive! I could feel her around me. The aroma of Murphy's Oil Soap often accompanies my grandmother when she's with me. Not this time, however. I only felt her. There were no parlor tricks or her usual barn-storming techniques she usually utilizes to snare attention. She was a bit of a ham in this world and, by golly, it's only been enhanced on the other side. She wants to get her point across and she will not stop until she succeeds. However, I can honestly say, she comes through with complete love and support. There is no doubt about that. She's been quite adamant about her desire to keep me on my spiritual path and she'll stop at nothing to make sure I do what I'm supposed to do.

"OK, Mamaw," I said aloud, "what do you want?"

I heard, or more accurately felt, "Talk to her."

Talk to her? I thought I was talking to her! I looked around and then I knew. My reason for being there in the first place… Her. I took a deep breath, centered myself, and asked, "Michelle? Are you here?" And, low and behold, she, indeed, was there, just behind me and to my left. Ya know what? I think this was the first time the woman ever did something she was asked to do.

In my mind's eye Michelle pointed to a tombstone ahead of me. "That's me," was all she said. I approached the marker and found this inscription:

> "I am not gone
> My soul lives on
> But in a better place."

I nodded and smiled. "I understand," I whispered. She then pulled me to another stone that read:

> "A soaring spirit
> A peaceful heart"

Then I 'heard' her say, "Now."

I had written a memorial for her in a newsletter catering to an organization in which we both held lifetime memberships. I had written, in part, "She was a classic tortured soul who, I pray, has found the peace she dodged so readily here." So, 'now', she has that peace I had written about. I could feel it, too. She was an intense woman—and some of that energy is still flowing strong—but there was a tranquility seeping through. She then directed me down the grassy hillside to a wonderfully decorated gravesite. This headstone bore the personal tender title of "My Beloved" and then this eloquent message:

> "Surrounded by this light of God
> In all his glory and grace.
> Life was a grand adventure!"

And then I heard her laugh. God, but she had the greatest laugh. It was loud, heartfelt and oh-so-very-real. That laugh was perhaps the most real thing about the girl. Yes, for her, life was truly a grand adventure. But, like an idiotic poster child for tom foolery, she made every action and thought a risk. Risks that she, more often times than not, lost. And it's because of those foolish risks that she now rests in the terrain of Oklahoma. As beautiful as these 'messages' were I had to blow the whole thing by letting our friend, Mr. Doubt, creep in the picture. Could I be leading myself around and just finding meaning behind random epitaphs? After all, how many graveyards are void of anything spiritual or moving? Give me a break. This could, after all, be the result of my overactive imagination. Right? Of course, right.

"Idiot."

Michelle would always call me an idiot when I would let my brain wander off in that kingdom of negative realism. For all of her shortcomings I will say that she had zero tolerance for self-pity or self-loathing in others. There was a tone that would emit from her; a sardonic pitch that was the audible embodiment of rolling your eyes. I don't know how she did it. In one word she could speak volumes. Sort of in the same way that a southerner can add eight syllables to the word 'shit'.

I was abruptly turned around as I heard, "Look!" At that moment I saw a bird resting on a bench. It was a bright surreal blue that nearly glowed. This bird was the brightest blue I had ever seen. As I took in this picture about 30 feet away from me, the bird soared into the air and was gone. I immediately hiked toward the bench, grass and sticks crunching beneath my feet. When I approached the small concrete bench I stopped— dare I say it?—dead in my tracks. The surface of the bench was covered in a wide variety of small, brightly colored stones.

Cobalt blue stones.

Right next to the bench was the final resting place of Dr. Henry Lee Wintz, Jr. According to the epitaph he also held the esteemed titles of 'Farmer, Philosopher, and Writer". It was one of the loveliest headstones I've ever seen. It depicted a large graphic representation of a tree on a hillside and it bore this quote:
> "Life is fascinating
> when one is conscious."

I didn't know what to say. I must have read that verse twenty times. It was her past and present summed up in seven words. At the risk of sounding redundant: 'wow'.

But we weren't done. Not but a long shot. Once again I found myself being directed to yet another spot. This time my energy was focused on the far end of this once small cemetery which, by now, seemed to be growing by leaps and bounds. Off in the distance I saw a grave that was more decorated than any I had seen. The only thing missing were search lights. So, still reeling from what I had just gone through, off I went to the adorned stone on the nearby horizon. When I reached our latest destination I felt my heart leap up into my throat. It was the grave of a baby; a sweet young boy who had passed away just days shy of 14 months of age. He had only been on this earth for this go around less than a year and a half but his family certainly went headfirst into truly celebrating his short but momentous life. Toys, flowers, personal items, and notes, among other things, were scattered about the plot of land. Nothing was held back. I could feel the joy and love despite the sorrow. How amazing! My eyes immediately went to the epitaph on the headstone that was larger than the child himself. But, of course, that is only in the physical sense. The stone read:

> "They say it takes a MINUTE to find a special person.
> An HOUR to appreciate them.
> A DAY to love them.
> But then an entire LIFETIME to forget them."

I chuckled and said, "I see you haven't lost your vanity over there, Michelle!"

I almost felt her slap me in the back of the head as she said, "That's for you... idiot!"

As I laughed—at her attitude or the absurdity of the overall experience—I noticed something else. Something that I had overlooked as I approached this message in marble. To the immediate right of the headstone was a simple yard ornament perched above the ground on a dowel rod; something you would see displayed in just about any average lawn or flower garden. It was a simple wooden bird. A simple brightly colored wooden bird. But it wasn't just any color, you know?

It was a bright, brilliant blue.

My laughter ceased almost instantaneously as the reality of the day hit me. And then I cried. Hard. Sure, I had cried when I lost Michelle so long ago. But that was over and done with by now. This was different. This was the first time I had actually cried since I had heard of her death. In her memorial I had written, "Personally, I am wrestling with exactly how I feel about her passing. I feel a need to grieve in some way but I am, at this writing, bewildered on how to go about it. There are no external tears." Well, that reaction, or lack there of, had certainly changed. This cry came from my heart and soul. I cried a cry of understanding. A cry of joy. Even a cry of love. But, more than anything, it was a cry of forgiveness… and release.

I had been toying with the idea of including some of Michelle's own words in this writing. I couldn't make up my own mind as to whether or not it was a good idea. As I wrote the above paragraph I received my answer. Near the end of my typing the above text I heard a loud crash behind me. I turned around to find that a book had fallen off a table. My cat, Max, was sound asleep on my bed so I can't blame him. There were no fans turned on and the windows were shut so I certainly can't point my finger at a breeze. What makes this so interesting is that the book fell directly on a box that just happened to contain Michelle's letters. Well, how about that? I opened the box and, right on top, I found the perfect words needed. Michelle was never lacking in personal commentary and I believe it's safe to say she hasn't changed. Well, at least not in that way.

I've learned a lot from her. And I'm quite stunned that I can say that with complete sincerity. When she left me I truly wanted to die. I was broken in a way that I had only experienced once before. I cursed her name as well as her memory. I wanted to literally forget everything about her—about us—just as she had obviously done. But now, with so much that has changed within my own mindset, I see the value of her in my life. I see the significance of the brevity of the good, the overwhelming tragedy of the bad and the ugliness of the soul searching. I see and understand that everything has a reason for being. Individuals walk in and out of our lives and none of them do so on a whim. Don't try to figure it all out—the mystery is half the fun—but make sure you take the time to be aware of those around you. Smile at the total stranger and move on to the next. The supply never ends.

Happy Birthday, Michelle. I love you and, more importantly, I offer you a simple, yet eloquent, thank you.

"This is THE all-time, numero uno letter of all time. I have NEVER been spoken to like this. Almost makes me afraid I'll disappoint you and lose you… There is nothing on the planet sexier than this letter. Nothing. Besides what it did to my soul, it actually affected me physically. I cannot elaborate on this detail without getting REALLY crass. Nuff said or your damn head won't fit through the doorways…"

Michelle
A letter to the author, 1997

"THE EAGLE HAS LANDED"

"Have faith. For faith will carry you above the clouds of doubt and despair providing a view that is more breathtaking than that of the highest eagle."

Robert

PERCEPTION IS EVERYTHING. If you don't believe me just let your eyes dance over the brilliantly mind-numbing artwork of E. C. Escher. Sometimes it's enough to drive you to drink. Is the glass half empty or half full? Or, in my case, it's simply not what I want because I am craving a cheeseburger. Yup, it's all a matter of perception. For example: there is an enormous difference between 'waking up on your own' and 'being awakened'. Light sleepers have it easy. It doesn't take much to get them to a waking state. A simple nudge will suffice. A slight shake of the shoulder or even a polite clearing of the throat will do the trick. Then there are people like me: the ones who can sleep through a hurricane while a marching band storms through the room blasting any given high school 'fight song' and not even flinch. To get me out of my hibernation I have to be bombarded with noise. Not once or twice but a multitude of times. It's the same process used to rouse me spiritually as well. Lately I've had my guides working overtime with chisels and mallets on my skull. They've been pounding day in and day out until I finally 'heard' them. They're either a relentless and devoted crew or they get paid a lot for overtime.

I had spent the first seven months of 2003 attending Psychic and Mediumship Development classes in Port Charlotte, Florida. Under the watchful eye of several skilled teachers, I discovered—along with my fellow 'classmates of life'—that my own abilities ran far deeper than I ever imagined. More importantly, I discovered the normalcy in what I do. We, as a whole, are psychic. It's not a matter of tapping into it as much as it is allowing yourself to tap into it and accepting it as a part of who and why you are. It's also great fun at parties and it keeps you entertained when the cable is out. Think of it as shadow puppets but without the physical exertion.

On the Saturday evening after our first class of the month it was customary for one of the instructors to host a group platform demonstration. This is a group reading before an audience of individuals nestling into overactive anticipation of hope and curiosity. The intimate group varies in size and can last anywhere from two to three hours (depending on the chattiness of the Spirits who join us for the evening's brouhaha). The one thing that is totally predictable with these school sessions is that the medium always picks up on my Spirit Guides. It's practically a tradition worthy of depiction by Norman Rockwell. While others are being comforted by their great Uncle Hector and Cousin Penelope, I'm getting descriptions of my spiritual entourage. Don't get me wrong: I have found a lot of comfort and validation in these readings. First and foremost, these experiences have proven to me that I am not schizophrenic. Being bombarded by a deluge of various energies and personalities is overwhelming when you're not accustomed to the idea. I have to admit that I was questioning my own sanity in the beginning. My first contact with my spirit guides was the equivalent of walking into a bar where everybody really does know your name.

This particular Saturday night was certainly no different. The medium paused in front of me and said, "I hate to do this but I'm seeing another guide." He took a deep breath as he said, "He's a Native American." I was told he was sitting on a rock overlooking the desert facing west. I chuckled and told him that I was planning a trip to Sedona, Arizona, later that month. I had not mentioned this trip to anyone. Well, no one on the physical plane anyway. The woman next to me started laughing. She was wearing a T-Shirt that read "SEDONA" in big bold block lettering. He also described, in great detail, a building that I would find while in Sedona. He said it was vital that I visit this place known only in his vision at this point. He described a large A-Frame log building with a green roof. The front would have very large windows—practically all glass. And there would be a lot of green surrounding it. He said I 'needed' to go there. Travel advice from the dead. Who knew?

I did some snooping on the Internet later that night and, low and behold, I found the building described to me. It was a place called "Michael's Vision" which was inspired by the Archangel Michael. I have a special connection to Michael (which is another story unto itself) so it all fell into place. I like to think of Archangel Michael as my personal archangel and I just happen to be generous enough to share him with the rest of the world. I also like to think that Michael pretends to find me funny. Yeaaaaaah. Sure he does.

I downloaded the photo from the website and showed it to the medium in residence the next morning. The first words out of his mouth were, "Are you going to buy that place?" I didn't tell him but the property was indeed up for sale. Location! Location! Location!

Just prior to my trip to Sedona one of my guides, Oliver—who is usually a man of few words—chimed in with one lone simple sentence that ended up dominating my every thought for over a week: "Eagles. Go with the eagles."

I asked, "What does THAT mean?"

He replied dryly, "You'll find out." I couldn't see him, of course, but I just knew he was smirking. Well, yee-haw, Katie bar the door 'cuz we're gonna have some fun now (said in my best trailer trash accent)!

I arrived in Sedona late on a hot Tuesday night in late July with nothing more than bewildered anticipation and a bottle of sun block. I didn't know what to expect and, frankly, I liked that idea. I've always hated planning and structure. I find the surrealistically whimsical approach to be best for me. Reality just bogs me down. Why balance my checkbook when I can create? Of course I was keeping an eye peeled for ANY references to eagles. I figured I would either find some earth shattering revelation connected to eagles or I would discover that Oliver has one perverse sense of humor. At that point in time both seemed utterly plausible.

Wednesday morning was spent at The Angel Valley Ranch in Sedona, which is home to the creator of "Michael's Vision" described earlier. My connection to the Archangel Michael took me to that place. I found myself quietly surrounded by the watchful protection of Michael for quite some time now and I'm always excited when other connections to him present themselves. Since Angel Valley was dropped in my lap and who am I to say 'no'? I was raised better than that and my Momma didn't raise no dummies. My grandparent's helped.

My guide on the ranch was the man who put the whole thing together and his name is—as hard as this may be to believe—Michael. Well, go figure. Michael, a slender man matching my 6' stature, has a very calming presence about him. It's as if he is 'tranquility' personified. He didn't even seem upset that I was nearly 30 minutes late. My tardiness was a result of my inability to find my own ass without a detailed map. I could get lost in a phone booth. Upon my arrival, and after introductions were made, we began walking. I assumed he knew where we were going so I blindly followed…the whole time mulling over whether I should leave a trail of bread crumbs.

I said to him, "I don't recall the last time I heard this much quiet."

"You don't have that in California," he said. It wasn't a question. It was a statement of fact that was based, I later found out, on personal experience.

"No, there isn't," I replied. "My idea of a quiet evening is when I don't have to listen to my neighbor's car alarm."

He smiled. "And yet you're still there." He led us to the left toward a small bridge. "You're the one in control, Charles."

"I like California," I said, "but I feel I need a change."

Again, he said matter-of-factly, "You're the one in charge." Then, out of the blue, Michael asked me, "What do you want, Charles?"

Silly mortal that I am, I replied, "I want to find out what's next in my spiritual growth."

Michael was kind enough to not laugh outwardly at me. We walked to a circle of rocks beneath a tree near the bridge and a stream. The tree seemed to envelope us within its limbs, like a mother protecting her young. We headed for a small circle of rocks near its trunk. He asked me to sit on a rock that 'spoke' to me. After pushing images of Jim Henson's 'Fraggle Rock' out of my mind I did so and he sat on my right at a 90 degree angle. We sat for about an hour-and-a-half 'just talking'. It was honestly better than any therapy that I'd ever had (and trust me that's been a LOT—not wanting to brag). After a while he asked me again, "What do you want?" He made me really think that time. After a pause I was surprised to find myself answering, "I want to feel." Michael smiled and said, "Now we're getting somewhere."

I turned myself off physically years ago. I became an extremely cerebral being at a very young age. For example, I don't FEEL that I'm in love. I KNOW I am in love. I don't FEEL tired. I KNOW I'm tired. Get it? There is a simple variation of the descriptions—replacing one word for another—but it is a massive difference. At the risk of repeating myself: perception is everything. It's also one of the few things that I simply do not think about. Physical emotions get in the way. Thoughts are far more logical. Not to mention far more satisfying.

Michael and I discussed the importance of the opening of the charkas, especially the heart. This is, of course, one of the two that I feel I have the most difficulties. I've noticed that even during chakra meditations my mind will wander off during the exercise covering the heart chakra: My conscious and subconscious working together to avoid that little demon. Nothing like teamwork, eh? When it's time to work on the heart chakra my mind goes off into an infomercial for the 'Amazing Space-Age Insta-Juicer 2000 Buttering Wand and Candle Maker' (or something equally intriguing) then returns in time for the throat chakra exercise.

"What excites you?" he asked. "What do you really love to do?"

"Obviously, I like drawing…" I began to say.

"Not 'like'. Listen to me: 'what do you really love to do?' See what I'm saying?" I nodded as he began telling me his own personal story. How he realized that he didn't really have anything in his life that 'excited' him. Once he realized this he ventured out on a cross-country trek. With what little he owned in his car and seven dollars in his pocket he drove from California to Pennsylvania. When he arrived in The Keystone State he had thirty-two dollars in his pocket…and a lot more faith. One tale in particular stuck with me: as he was driving through one state he noticed he was not only nearly out of gas but in the middle of nowhere, population zero. He kept saying to himself, 'I need money. I need money. Where am I going to get money?' Finally, he said he heard a 'chorus of angels' say to him, "You dummy! You don't need money! What you need is gas!"

Again, it's all a matter of perception. I have to admit I'm a bit jealous. I really would love to have a chorus of angels call me a dummy.

He realized they were right. Once he made peace with that idea he came upon a farm house just off the road. He said he considered it a miracle. He pulled into the road leading to the home and prayed for 'the kindness of strangers'. The farmer had seen him turn onto his property and was waiting for him. Michael explained he was almost out of gas and definitely out of money and hoped that the man could spare him a couple gallons so he could continue his journey. Without hesitation the man began filling the fuel tank from his own supply. After a few minutes of friendly banter the man asked Michael, "What does your gauge say now?" The tank was full. The man said, "Now that didn't take long, did it?"

"Like I told you, Charles, you're the one in charge," Michael said. "There comes a time in your life when you need to change patterns. You must want this. I faced that moment myself and I just told the universe 'I'm done!' and I meant it. When you accept that you are at that place in your life the Universe will work with you and in the time frame you desire. Do you want to change in a week? A month? A year? It's up to you." He smiled knowingly. "Finding what it is that truly excites you is part of that change. Find it and do it. Stop saying what you think people want you to say and say what you feel."

There's that infernal "F" word again.

And then that bastard had the nerve to ask just one more time: "What do you want?" I briefly considered knocking him in the head with a Twinkie and running for my car in a flurry of dust and gravel. However, my disdain for physical exertion, combined with my overall almost religious devotion to mass produced cream-filled pastry, prevented me from taking that blasphemous route. So I had no option but to tell the truth. I said, "I want to own what I feel."

There. I said it. Happy now?

Michael sent me out on my own to 'just go where your excitement takes you.' No expectations, no rules to go by. Just do…whatever. As I started off on my odd quest Michael asked, "What brought you here?" Without thinking I replied, "I'm here on a wing and a prayer." He smiled and said, "That's all you really need."

After climbing to the top of a hill I was most pleased to see that I could appreciate the beauty all around me before dying of a massive combination heat stroke and coronary. I decided to do some breathing exercises and meditations. I then announced to the Universe that upon completion of this exercise I would have a better insight to this eagle 'dilemma'. Once the exercises had concluded I opened my eyes and what did I see but an AIRBORNE EXPRESS van driving through the valley below. As is my custom in these situations, I simply burst out laughing.

After traipsing around in 108 degree heat I found a most inviting creek. Without rationalizing in any way, I wandered out into the middle of it, beneath a waterfall, and plopped myself down in it. It was WONDERFUL! I just sat there for about an hour just letting the waterfall soak me from head to toe. So, as this 'city boy' was communing with nature he was totally unaware that the contents of his back pack were being ruined. This included his small art portfolio that he had placed in there and had conveniently forgotten about its existence. Twelve years of work GONE.

The screaming that came with the discovery of this mistake later in the day has been rumored to set off seismographs in a 550 mile radius. Tides altered. Animals ran from the forest in a panic. Natives in the mountains made up songs about it. A group of tourists were lost in an avalanche in the Grand Canyon. However, they were all lawyers so no one really noticed, or cared, that they were missing.

Was this a sign that I would NOT be moving to Sedona? Was it a sign to say that I was there to grow spiritually and not focus on my artwork? Perhaps it was meant as more proof that I need to change everything. Or it could be just my own obliviousness to the reality that I've created around me. A friend of mine told me 'Sometimes we have to throw out what we think we know in order to really learn something.' You know what I learned? I learned that I was pissed! How's that for a friggin' life lesson?

I tried meditating Wednesday night but had no success. My mind was everywhere… except where it should have been. My first full day in Sedona had proven to be, for the most part, a major disaster (or so I thought at that moment in time). I had originally planned to have lunch with a woman named Heather that afternoon. She is a fellow artist and psychic who also happens to be the niece of the very first psychic I ever met. I had been talking with Heather's Aunt Donna for a decade yet she NEVER had the urge to speak of Heather until I had made my plans to visit Sedona. The fact that I had an interest in psychic phenomenon coupled with my being an artist was never enough for Donna to drag Heather into the conversation. But, once I made the plans, Donna just couldn't shut up about Heather. I couldn't just shrug it off as a mere coincidence.

However, as things were going from bad to worse, Heather and I did not get together as planned. I spent more time than originally planned at the ranch so, by the time I called her Wednesday evening, she seemed 'disinterested'. She said she would call me back later that night and we'd finalize plans for the next afternoon. The phone did not ring again the rest of the night.

The next morning I was livid. Tossing aside the wealth of self reflection I had attained at the Ranch on Wednesday I was considering this trip to be nothing short of a farce. I was disgusted beyond belief. My life's work was ruined. Heather, who I thought would be a great connection for me, was a no-show. I was spending money that I did not have. I exclaimed, "SCREW IT" (in far more descriptive terms than I care to post here) and decided right then and there that I was going home. If I could not get my ticket changed at no charge I was going to just live at the airport until Saturday and sulk.

"Pity Party of One? Your table is ready!"

I'd had it. I was walking away and not looking back. The instant I made that poorly chosen mock-decision the telephone rang. It was Heather apologizing for not getting back to me the night before and asking if we could meet on Friday instead of Thursday. I took a deep breath, kicked myself for doubting and enthusiastically agreed. I hung up the phone and just muttered to anyone within earshot, "Well, I guess you told me, huh?"

There's no way to prove it, of course, but I'm convinced Archangel Michael was, at that very moment, muttering something along the lines of, "Neener neener boo boo." Remember that whole "I like to think Michael finds me funny" comment earlier? I hope he does, too.

I walked down the street to a local Denny's for lunch. It would be rather absurd to walk down the street to a non-local Denny's wouldn't it? "I'm going to Albuquerque for a bite. See you on Thursday!" It just doesn't work. I was served by a lovely young lady named Brooke who was in possession of one of the most radiant smiles I've ever seen. I ordered a grilled chicken sandwich with apple sauce instead of fries. Brooke asked, "Are you on that weird Atkins Diet?" I looked at her, shaking my head 'no', totally bewildered how anyone can accuse me of being on any kind of diet. She said, "A lot of people come in here that are on the Atkins Diet and they will get applesauce instead of fries. Then they will eat the burger but not the bread, ya know?"

I smiled and said, "I just happen to really like applesauce."

She smiled and said, "Well that's a better excuse than being on Atkins! That's just wrong!" I had to admit I agreed with her. Then she asked, "Are you traveling?"

"You have no idea," I said dryly.

"Where are you headed?"

"Here." I paused for a moment. "Sedona. Not Denny's." Sometimes it's best to clarify.

She laughed and asked, "Where are you from?"

Chatty little thing, isn't she? I told her I was currently hailing from southern California where everything should be stamped AS SEEN ON TV.

"That's funny. Most people leave here to visit there instead of the other way around. What brought you here?"

My first instinct was to say "an airplane" but opted against it. I thought, "oh what the hell?" and I said, "You could say I'm here on a spiritual pilgrimage. No real rhyme or reason. I'm just traveling on a wing and a prayer."

She said, "Oh, really?"

Then I decided to 'go for broke'. I said, "I've discovered I have this wacky ability to talk to the dead." I paused. "They talk to me, I talk to them, and wackiness ensues." I looked at her fully expecting her to scream "HERETIC" at the top of her lungs while dousing me in holy water. I had a straw poised for action just in case. I was parched.

She flashed that smile and said, "Oh, I understand. My whole family is like that."

I was dumbfounded. I've had several friends who have packed up their old kit bag and got out of Dodge when they found out I was getting into mediumship. I've even had one in particular tell me that she was afraid I was losing my mind. She went on to tell me she would do 'anything' within her power to get me help if it got 'out of hand'. And here was a total stranger telling me it was as normal as ordering applesauce in place of fries. Sometimes you just have to change your diet. Replacing fries with applesauce doesn't take away from the meal as a whole but merely changes it. The nutrition is there—even enhanced—and it just takes some time to stop craving the fries. You don't have to stop eating all together. Just alter your diet. As Michael told me: "I'm done!" I never knew wisdom could be found in a Denny's. Gum under the tables, sure, but not insight.

Despite the deluge of self validations being strewn about, I was still no closer to solving this mysterious eagle reference. I was, of course, getting quite frustrated over the whole thing. Have you, by chance, picked up on the fact that I'm just not patient? Rumor has it that patience is a virtue. I'm OK with that theory providing that the virtue comes 'round the mountain quickly. Needless to say I keep my guides quite busy hurling debris at me every few minutes. I like to think of myself as their personal workout regime.

I gave the menu at Denny's a quick once-over to make sure they didn't offer a 'Batter Dipped Eagle' luncheon special. No such luck. Obviously I wasn't supposed to get all of my answers at America's Favorite Diner. It's a good thing that I didn't because there's was a Denny's just around the corner from where I lived at the time. I would have been ticked having spent all that time and money traveling to Sedona for a blue plate special of perception when I could have just walked down the block. I will admit, however, that the timing of Heather's call had truly convinced me that I was supposed to be in Sedona. Lord, but I'm easy.

Later that evening I hopped in my rental and headed out to a grocery store. I was craving cantaloupe. Hey, it happens. I like healthy food if it tastes good! On a whim I had this desire to listen to a CD entitled "Live at Blues Alley" by Eva Cassidy. Eva was a extraordinarily gifted singer from the Washington, DC, area who left this world far too soon. She possessed a voice that can literally bring me to my knees. I'm not much of a fan of music in general; I listen to very little. But Eva is different. Her voice touches my soul—it hits home—pure and simple. Without thinking I slid the silver disk into the CD player and found myself chuckling over the first track: "Cheek to Cheek". I'm on a spiritual pilgrimage and I'm hearing the voice of an angel singing "Heaven…I'm in heaven…". Ya gotta love it. The second track, entitled "Stormy Monday", began playing and I didn't think anything about it at first. Suddenly, as I'm sitting at a traffic light, ONE lyric jumped out at me: "The eagle flies on Friday." I just stared at the console and at that moment I knew Heather would have the key to this grating eagle reference. She had, just a few hours earlier, changed our clandestine meeting from Thursday to Friday. Was this divine intervention or just my desire to dump the responsibility in Heather's lap? To be honest, either solution worked very well for me at that point.

As I pulled into the parking lot of the market, still chuckling in awe over "the eagle will fly on Friday", another track had started. This one was entitled "People Get Ready." It starts with these lyrics:

> "People get ready
> There's a train a comin'..."

Then it offers up this little slap-in-the-face snippet:

> "All you need is faith
> To hear the diesel hummin'"

The instant the second line was sung a train whizzed by along the track directly across the road blowing its whistle. I started to laugh and just muttered, "smart ass" to the cosmos. "Oh, yea," I thought shaking my head, "I'm gonna pay for that one later."

While in this grocery store I found a section displaying a wide selection of religious candles. Saint Francis and Mother Teresa stuffed right in there between Spam and Mrs. Butterworth. How handy. Save your soul, grab a bite, and you're on your way. You have to love the convenience of it all. And, low and behold, amidst these candles encased in what resembled tall and skinny drinking glasses, was one for my pal, the Archangel Michael. It was only 99 cents. I figured Mikey was worth a buck so I put it in my basket next to my cantaloupe and Caesar salad... the whole time praying I would not somehow get them confused at the peak of my feeding frenzy.

Thursday night I went through my meditations and this time had success. In addition to calling in my usual entourage, I asked to speak directly with the Archangel Michael. Why not, right? You never know until you try. Within moments I felt a very strong energy around me; it was a force unlike any I have experienced so far. It was very strong, even authoritative. Not threatening by any means but I was given a feeling of a higher presence that had a definite purpose. Most importantly it was absolutely not Robert, my Master Guide (or any other member of my spiritual entourage for that matter). There was definitely a new kid on the block. I was immediately lead to my laptop. While I normally take pen in hand to transcribe these messages from upon high, I knew that this had to be typed. The energy was too strong for my mere hand. There was no way my penmanship could keep up with this intensity while still remaining legible. I sat down at the keyboard and this is the conversation that flowed like wildfire from my fingertips:

What message do you have for me?

"I come in love, understanding, benevolence, trust and truth. Be steadfast in your faith, Charles. It will not let you down. On a wing and a prayer you are perched and shall not fall. It is God's love that never falters. It is your love that He seeks. You have offered it to Him unconditionally and he is stronger for it. Yes, God 'needs' your Love. You were made in God's own image–does He not feel as you? Do you not need the love of others? Of yourself? God is no different. You have not quite grasped the concept of 'Your God Self'. God IS within you and you are within God. Between heaven and earth is the almighty love of God and Man, permanently binding them together as one. Do not ignore the greatness within you for God has never ignored it. Accept it, Charles! Own it! Be the man that you are, not the man you THINK you are. Your reality is within your hands. Allow it to breathe and thrive. Like a butterfly let it soar swiftly, elegantly and with beauty. Open your palm, Charles, and release the butterfly from its cocoon. You are protected, you are growing. THAT is what you FEEL, Charles. What you perceive as doubt is CHANGE. You do not yet fully understand what is happening so you 'naturally' fear. You must admonish the fear; beseech it to leave you and, in its place, you will find God's unconditional love. Within that love you will find AND understand the truth. The truth being YOU; not an illusion but the real thing."

I worry about taking pride in my abilities.

"It is not a sin to be proud. Are you using your abilities for personal gain? Are you using them to mislead others?"

If I do this for a living I will be gaining from it.

"But is that the MAIN reason?"

No.

"There, my friend, is your answer."

It's hard to let go of insecurities.

"Insecurities are not truths. The truth is within the light. If you walk into a darkened room you are unsure of what lies ahead, correct? Once you turn the light on you know where to step. The trick is finding the light switch. YOU have found that switch, Charles. It's in the same place each time you step into the room. Why do you ignore its very existence yet dwell on the existence of non-truths? Old habits die hard BUT they are replaced by the reality of God within you, your life, your surroundings…need I go on? God IS everywhere, Charles. Even in that darkened room you enter with such trepidation. Reach inside, turn on the light, walk where you know you should tread. The furniture may be moved but the path will always be seen. Have faith. As the staff in your hand steadies you over the rough terrain, so shall your faith. The journey will grow within you but shall always be clearly marked. OPEN YOUR EYES! Trust in yourself and KNOW God will never falter or leave your side. Be one with God as you go with God. In peace, in strife, God is there."

And then 'it' was gone. I asked a couple of times just who I was talking to and I was answered by silence. I know, in my heart, it was the Archangel Michael. I asked to speak with him therefore my faith tells me that is exactly what happened. Once I added Michael to my collection of spiritual connections I felt compelled to ask the hotel management for a special group rate for my room.

Simply put: Friday could not get here fast enough.

I drove into Sedona along AZ 89A taking in the breathtaking scenery. I stopped frequently at various 'scenic overlooks' along the route. As I was pulling out of the first tourist trap overlook I found myself behind a green SUV (like Elvis they are everywhere!). Painted on the back of that vehicle was a dream catcher with a soaring eagle in the middle of it. When I pulled out into the regular flow of traffic I saw the shadow of an eagle flying overhead cross the pavement before me. Slap me in the face again, why don'cha?

I met Heather at a Mexican Restaurant in the heart of the tourism that is Sedona. After proper introductions (which, among artistic types, can really be just about anything) we sat down and she immediately began discussing the tarot. Thankfully I was donning my blue sunglasses (a must for any fashionable medium don'cha know) so she couldn't see my eyes widening to the size of half dollars. I said nothing but I was thinking "Well, son of a bitch".

I'm widely known for my Mastery of the English Language. Yuh-huh, I shor is…

I have a major blockage to the tarot. I've attempted 'fiddling' with them, for lack of a better term, with no success. I run into walls and obstacles over and over again. I can't grasp them—or so I want to think. I would have more luck if I tried to read lint. One of my guides, Pamela, is here, she claims, to help me with the tarot. As I see it dear old Pamela needs to sit down for a long one-on-one with Saint Jude for this little miracle to transpire. My learning the tarot is about as hopeless as finding a Hooter's in the middle of the desert. (And I have looked!)

Oddly, as I run like a madman from the tarot, I find it being thrust in my face with more regularity than the best of bran could offer. I have insisted, time and time again, that I can't read the damn cards! And yet I have two decks, six books on the subject and even an Angel Oracle Card deck. Oh, yea, I'm 'running' from it all right. And here's Heather, a total stranger, talking about those infernal cards the instant we meet. My guides must take turns driving yet another spike into my cranium.

Amidst her structured speech she suddenly stopped and explained, "When I went to bed last night I just knew I had to talk to you about the tarot." I just laughed. I explained the whole 'tarot blockage' that I have and how I seem to be the only one who sees this impasse. I added, "My guides keep bringing it back into my life. Now, if they could just bring me a Hooter's cheerleader, I'd be fine."

Heather laughed. Thankfully.

Later in the conversation she said, "You know, just before I read your email about the eagles, I was having these random thoughts about eagles. Isn't that weird?" Before I could respond a flash of realization swept across her face. "Have you been to the Chapel of the Holy Cross?"

I shook my head. "Never heard of it," I said.

She went on to explain that it was a chapel designed by Frank Lloyd Wright and built into the rocks overlooking Sedona. She leaned into me and said, "There is a rock formation up there that looks exactly like a giant eagle head. You know how you can look at some formations and say, 'oh yea that could be an eagle or it could be a Buick'? That's not the case with this one. It really looks like an eagle!" She emphasized each syllable of that last sentence with a series of rapid-fire pokes in my upper arm. She then leaned back and said matter-of-factually, "You have to go there." Since I have no will power of my own I caved and readily agreed to visit the Chapel of the Holy Cross later that day.

After meandering through a few art galleries, Heather and I parted company and I headed back to my Ranger. As I entered the sparsely populated parking lot I stopped dead in my tracks. Parked a measly four empty spaces away from my vehicle was a Hooter's Calendar truck with photos of Hooter's girls plastered all over it. My jaw fell open, swaying in the desert breeze. If my eyes had grown any wider they would have merged together to give me that dashing Cyclops look that any unibrow would envy. Then, as is my custom, I dropped to my knees laughing in hysterics. Are my guides on top of things, or what? Now where did I put that tarot deck...?

Along the road leading out of Sedona, and toward the Chapel of the Holy Cross, there is an art gallery that has a massive sculpture of an eagle erected outside of the building. Suddenly eagles were everywhere! I made a left onto Chapel Road, parked the gray Ranger, and proceeded to hike up the path to the church overlooking the panoramic scenery below. Along the pathway up to the church there is a statue depicting St. Francis of Assisi, another saint that has been connected with me by other mediums. Yet another indication I was, indeed, on the right path. But why did it have to be so steep? I think all paths should have moving sidewalks and/or escalators. But that's just me.

Once I reached the top (still bewildered why I hadn't melted like the Wicked Witch of the West) I found myself being physically turned clockwise until I was facing a stone eagle head which overlooked the back of the chapel. I was immediately bombarded by a massive surge of energy that led me to a small wall. I was physically turned around, and 'pushed' gently down to a sitting position. Then I heard "Shhhhhhh." I tried to 'listen' when a gaggle of tourists approached chattering about the heat, their bunions, the hilarity of their recently purchased I'M WITH STUPID t-shirts and other such topics of disinterest. I got up and walked inside the sanctuary seating myself in the last of the seven benches masquerading as pews. Of course the benches were out of the sunlight so I was happy. I would have sat on a pile of rattle snakes as long as they weren't in the heat. I had lived in the Washington, DC, area for ten years so I'm immune to the bite of poisonous snakes. Wow! Enlightenment AND political commentary wrapped up in one saucy burrito? What a bargain!

There was a small group of individuals sitting in the sanctuary. Some kneeling, some sitting in quiet reflection and others just damned thrilled to be out of the sunlight. It was like I was sitting between a colony of Christians and a roving band of vampires. A description, I believe, that can adequately sum up any family reunion. A variety of hymns were playing over the internal PA system. I calmed and centered myself, closed my eyes, took three deep breaths and heard, "What are you going to write?" I was confused by this comment. Again, "What are you going to write?"

I replied, "I don't know what you mean."

Again, but this time far more insistent, "What are you going to write?"

I thought for a moment. I had no idea there would be a pop quiz on this trip. I was the one always asking questions and now the tables were turned. I was paying the price for the manifestation of the Hooter's truck. "I guess something that will help others learn..." I uttered without an ounce of conviction.

"RIGHT!" I 'heard'... or dare I say, 'felt'? "In order to teach you must learn more, open your mind to more possibilities." Then 'he' went on to give me a 'polite' lecture on Christianity. I have this habit of butchering the religion at every turn. I never liked it much and I tend to rag on it a lot. "There is nothing wrong with Christianity," I was told. "The problem lies within the malpractioners of it. Remember that." Of course, I had to admit he was right. "In order to teach you must free your mind of unnecessary baggage and weight for that will only limit you. Prejudice and ignorance have no place in the classroom. Do not forget 'life' is a classroom."

I asked, "OK. Who ARE you?" Here I am being handed profound information and I'm wondering who's talking to me. Am I a butthead or what?

"I am known as The One Who Soars with Eagles."

"But what is your name?" Refer to the 'butthead' remark above.

"You would not be able to pronounce it," he replied. He was not being condescending by any means. He was very matter-of-fact and I believed him. After a slight pause he then said simply, "Go in peace."

Just as I was reeling from that experience I suddenly 'knew' the title of my book: 'On a Wing and a Prayer'. Well, go figure. Once that dawned on me the PA began blaring another hymn in the Heaven's Top 40: "The Old Rugged Cross". This hymn "coincidentally" was my favorite when I was a kid. I admit that was pretty cool although I was more impressed with the Hooter's truck. Once again please reference the earlier 'butthead' statement.

I left Sedona not as a new man but as an awakened man. As I pulled out of the chapel I saw an eagle flying high in the south western sky, just swooping down, left and right, going with the wind. It looked random but yet, at the same time, meticulous, refined and with self-assured purpose. I pulled off the road, put the truck in park, and just watched this majestic creature dancing in the sky. Many people sped by me, either immune or indifferent to their surroundings, as I absorbed every movement of this seemingly private viewing. "Thank you," I whispered to no one in particular as I leaned on the steering wheel and just gazed, smiling, ever upward.

And so it began…

"Love Lives"

"I have found the paradox, that if you love until it hurts, there can be no more hurt, only more love."

Mother Teresa

I AM THE FIRST TO ADMIT I HAVE A LOT OF ODD IDIOSYNCRASIES. No shock there, right? I cannot pour milk over my bowl of Frosted Mini-Wheats until I turn all of the little morsels frosting-side-up. I hate bare walls. Always have. So I have framed pieces of art and photographs plastered all over mine. What's so weird about that? They must be exactly 72" from the floor. And, for the record, they're equidistantly spaced. I tend to have a wee bit of an obsession with order. Yet, whenever I am working on a book, whether writing or illustrating, I never, EVER, work in sequence. I'm a walking paradox, yet I have no boat, let alone two. (Think about that one and get back to me…) Upon reflection, each and every one of those peculiarities makes my talking to the dead seem pretty gosh-darn normal.

One item from my collection of quirks does tend to leap out off the psychiatrist's pad, though. Every night, when I first go to bed, I always say, "I love you" aloud. No idea why, really. I don't know why it started or how. I'm not even sure when. It's just there. I don't even have a clue as to whom I'm saying it. I could be saying it to God or Spirit, depending on your preferred terminology. Perhaps I'm saying it to a lover, past, present and/or future. Maybe I'm saying it to myself. No clue. Yet, every night, as my head and pillow become one, I blurt it out. No rhyme or reason, yet it feels out of place if I don't.

Those three little words can have a massive impact, especially if whispered at the right time. Those words can ring through long corridors in your mind for decades. My dear friend, Leigh, and I always ended every conversation with those words. And, of course, when we were together, we did not go to bed without saying them just one more time. So, I can take great comfort and joy in the fact that our last words to one another, just one lone week before her abrupt passing, were "I love you."

My beloved Aunt Ruth's last act of coherence, just before she slipped away nearly a year ago, was telling each of us sitting with her those same magical words. Trust me when I tell you that is a moment in time that her son, daughter-in-law, sister and slightly anal-retentive nephew will never forget. And, of course, we returned those very same words in kind. You can't ask for a whole lot more, you know?

To this day, some thirty-odd years later, I can still vividly recall the euphoria of exchanging those words with my first real girlfriend for the very first time. Giddiness isn't the same without a big goofy grin implanted on your face for days on end, you know? I hope she can still reflect back on that time with the same soft-hearted mindset as I do. However, she's pretty old now and probably senile. (God, I hope Dar's not reading this…with her trifocals. Oh, yeah, I'm a dead man now!)

Of course, keep in mind I offer those same three words to a wide variety of people in my life: the waitress who brings me cheesecake, the pizza delivery guy, anyone who gives me cookies (unless they contain raisins or coconut). The list is quite long. Hell, I propose marriage to anyone who pulls their car out of a spot so I can park there. I just toss those 'I love you's' around all willy-nilly like fertilizer. There's an image for you. Of course, if you think about it, that reflection is quite right. Sharing an 'I love you' in hopes it will take root and flourish, spreading like wild flowers in the wind. Makes sense to me. But, then again, so does hanging things on a wall exactly six feet from the floorboards. I'm not really a good gauge for some things.

There are two things I truly adore when connecting with the energy of someone who has crossed over to the other side. The first is whenever they embarrass the sitter. Yes, I said it. I get the biggest kick out of it. They will, with great regularity, bring up some hysterically funny incident that the sitter (almost) wishes time would forget. The look of shock followed by red-faced embarrassment is priceless. But what REALLY puts the icing on the cake is the smile that follows. A smile of recollection, reconnection and reassurance. Of course, the dead guy gets the biggest laugh out of it. I mean, seriously, what are you going to do to 'em? They're dead for cryin' out loud!

The second item on my two-item list is the insistence of the love between the one in spirit and the one sitting before me. Sure, when you get a message, you expect the classic, "I love you". It's a nearly worn out cliché. In all honesty, this Universal Message never gets old. Each of you knows it so why roll your eyes and deny it? Each and every Spirit that comes through is doing so out of love for you. Whether they say, "I love you!" or if they discuss the latest remodeling of your kitchen. Their very presence in your life, both then and now, is out of love. Eat your heart out, Hallmark. While you insist on a lone day in February, Spirit offers it 24/7 for a full 365. Hell of a marketing campaign if you ask me.

Oh, yeah, I hear you. "How is talking about my kitchen a sign of love?" Simple, ya big doofus. By talking about your kitchen they're telling you that they are still active in your life. They are letting you know that they're there for the big and the mundane, the highs and the lows, and everything else in-between, just as in their physical life. Some say "I love you" in different ways. Words, actions, thoughts... most commonly it's a combination of those and more. A peck on the cheek, a tousle of your hair, a hug, a spin across the dance floor, preparing your favorite meal... the list goes on and on.

How do YOU let someone know you love them? Hmm? How do YOU let others know you care? Take a moment and think about it. For example, my uncle and I merely had to shake hands while placing our free hand on the shoulder of the other.

That's all we needed. He's been gone now for 30 years and, let me tell you, I still miss those handshakes from time to time. There was so much wrapped in those simple actions. It was a genuine fondness, friendship and love. I know he's still with me—that won't change—but, every now and again, the physical side longs for what was. And that's perfectly normal. You can't risk losing the connection to your physical side, even the part that brings up tears. It's all connected so allow it to flow. What is sad today can lead to happiness tomorrow.

The love of, and for, your loved ones is still with you. Why? Because THEY are still with you. Sure, it's not the way we prefer or are even accustomed to, but they're still with us. Love does not die, love does not fade or go away. It lives, it thrives and it never asks why. I'll remember that the next time someone brings me a slab of cheesecake.

I would love to exchange an 'I love you' with Leigh again. I would cherish hearing Aunt Ruth say, "I love you, honey" just once more. I'd like the chance to tell Dar that I love her, for the sake of honoring the moment that was, without her slapping me in the back of the head with her trifocals. And, I can—and do—each night when I go to bed. I release those positive words into the ethers knowing they will, somehow, find their way to the souls who need it most, myself included.

In case you don't hear it tonight, I love you.

"IT'S ALL IN THE CARDS"

"A deck of cards fans out. You do the same, you know? Your aura, your energy, fans out to others. The people will reach in and pull out what they need from you. But always remember this: what they take is only what YOU freely give."

Pamela

OF ALL OF THE INQUIRIES I RECEIVE, I have to say that the topic of Spirit Guides is in the top three. I have a very strong, and obvious, working relationship (or on-going feud, depending on the day) with my ensemble of enlightened ectoplasm. I've been fortunate enough to have connected clearly with them from the very beginning. While it seemed like a grand idea at the time, I'm willing to bet they're kicking themselves now. Some of my Guides tend to be more prominent than the others. You know this just by skimming over my Facebook page or thumbing through my book, DAILIES. Some just seem more talkative. So I thought I would begin writing about some of my 'lesser known' Guides. They all assist me in my readings, meditations, writings—not to mention that daily routine you hear so much about—so I don't want to give the impression that some are more important than others. There's no Warren G. Harding or Chester Alan Arthur in my line up. Each stands out in their own way with their own Divine Purpose. The one common denominator is they have all improved on their golf swing whacking their clubs up against my cement abutment of a skull. God love 'em.

In April, 1909, Pamela Coleman Smith was commissioned by A.E. Waite to design arguably the most recognizable tarot deck in history: The Rider-Waite-Smith Deck (now known as The

Rider-Waite Deck). At the time it consisted of 80 drawings and by 1911 black and white prints would appear with Waite's book entitled The Pictorial Key to the Tarot. Thus ends the lesson.

In my early days of development, I was introduced to a new Spirit Guide by the name of Pamela. She was my fifth spiritual sidekick right after Christopher, my Tibetan Monk with ADHD (Ya can't make this stuff up, people). Pamela gave me a swift glimpse of her physical appearance, like Christopher, in the very beginning. I saw a young woman with olive skin, dark eyes & hair, with full lips. She was dressed, in my best description, like a gypsy. I almost expected her to conjure up Larry Talbot. I'm also convinced she is an avid smoker but she denies it. She insists she is a reformed smoker. Oh, c'mon, Pamie. You can't be helped until you're honest with yourself first. Ahem.

She informed me that her role was to help me learn the Tarot. I knew nothing of the cards at the time and just accepted it for what it was. Our relationship began as a shipwreck beaten on the rocks and escalated rapidly downhill at a heart-skipping pace. Tarot and I did NOT get along from the git-go. The deck and I just didn't mesh. I would stare at the cards and they simply stared right back at me. It was about as uncomfortable as an obligatory holiday family dinner.

Poor Pamela's pet project was pretty much a pratfall. Of course, in those early days of my development, Pamela was still a wide-eyed entity chock full of determination and hope. Now, thanks to me, she's bitter, broken and buzzing about bygone days of bliss. But she stays because she either has no place else to go or she's a masochist. Probably a little bit of both.

Yeaaaaa… she's gonna use my head for badminton practice for that one.

At one point along the way I found out about the artist of the Tarot, Pamela Coleman Smith. Needless to say, my jaw came crashing down on the tile. Could MY Spirit Guide be THE

Pamela? I have to admit I was both impressed and intimidated. It seemed for a moment that Spirit had brought out the Big Guns. I had a sudden feeling I needed to really toe the line. And nothing creeps me out more than obligation. I put it out there and, in an automatic writing session, she answered my question. In her already familiar, snarky tone she wrote, "No, but I had you going there for a minute, didn't I?" It was at that point that I proposed marriage, as is my custom in such situations.

Her moniker provided me with an amazing validation. Of all the names I could have been given, I receive the very name of THE illustrator of THE Tarot Deck. Coincidence? Not by a long shot. The odds are just too high for that to even be considered.

She is brutally direct and she refuses to put up with my crap. She calls me on it all the time and, honestly, I'm grateful that she does. I can't get away with anything with her. Excuses are unacceptable, end of story. I recall, once upon a time, when I attempted to take a beginners Tarot class in Anaheim. The class description boasted it was for fledgling amateurs who didn't know squat about the Tarot. LIES! ALL LIES! It seemed to me that everyone in that class, minus myself of course, had been reading the Tarot prior to leaving the womb. While I was only comfortable with knowing which side of the card to have face-up, everyone else was tapping into the deep corners of the Universe and revealing the secrets of life to any and all.

"I got a rock."
Charlie Brown

It was a four week class and I lasted two of them. After that first night I was enraged. I stormed out of the building like a rabid dog. I was storming down the street toward my car, ranting and raving the whole time. I went on and on about what a joke this was, how I was too stupid to understand this undecipherable language, and on and on and on. When I

FINALLY had to pause to take a breath, I heard Pamela oh-so-very-clearly ask, "Are you through?"

I hate when a woman asks me that.

Undeterred in my own lavish self-pity, I screamed, "How can I expect to see anything hidden in a damn card when I can't even see YOU?"

Keep in mind this conversation was out-loud on a busy, bustling street around nine o'clock at night. Of course, it IS Southern California so passers-by were assuming I was either talking on a hands-free phone or I was schizophrenic. Both are equally common out here and, for the record, I lean more toward the latter of the two.

Pamela, in her already familiar Angelic tone oozing with love, replied, "Don't give me that whinny 'I can't see you' shit. Do you want to do this or not?"

Yes, dear.

Pamela realized that this relationship was just not working. I'm no stranger to that, but that's beside the point. So, like any adaptable enlightened being, she switched gears. She began working with my understanding of symbolism in general. My readings are often a rapid-fire bombardment of images, one after another, like psychic flashcards. It's a quick form of shorthand that is designed to keep my physical mind happy to have a puzzle to solve while my connection to Spirit gets to jump over the fence of so-called reality in order to 'hear' the true message. After that slap in the back of my noggin, the clarity of the symbols has been staggering. It was as if I had learned a new language almost overnight. I don't know how she did it—what wires she crossed—but, by gum by golly, it worked. I find myself connecting dots that don't seem to be related…until I discover that missing key. Once that key turns in the lock a whole new level of understanding is revealed to all parties involved. And, honestly, it's a trip.

She has also helped greatly with my seemingly natural connection to oracle cards. Why I can't relate to the Tarot is beyond me. I'm sure it's my own mental block at this point (a polite expression for 'bull-headed flibbertigibbet'). I've just accepted it for whatever it is. I suppose I should give Pamela credit for the Oracle Connection, but the last thing I want to do is to give my Entourage a reason to feel good about Themselves.

Pamela is the one who prompted me to officially offer Oracle Card readings in addition to my regular sessions. Prompted, by the by, is a refined euphemism for 'bullying', in case you're wondering. She is also the Mastermind behind my occasional "Card of the Day" postings on Facebook, Twitter and Instagram (for the 9 of you who follow all three venues). On occasion, whenever she is feeling like banging her head against a cement barrier, she attempts to sneak a Tarot lesson or two in the mix. And, as expected, it's never really met with great verve.

I bought a Rider-Waite deck several years ago. Even after discovering my ineptitude with the cards, I kept them around like that odd uncle that no one really understands but, yet, you find comforting to invite to Christmas dinner, even if only for comedic relief. That's MY goal in life, BTW. I placed the deck of cards in a wooden box and kept it on my altar. A photo of Pamela Coleman Smith stands guard on top of it. I like to have little trinkets, if you will, to represent my Guides on my altar. I don't have items for all of them—yet—but I've found things for a little over half. It helps, in my mind's eye, to solidify their presence in a physical sense.

Over the years, and throughout a handful of relocations crisscrossing the country, they ended up packed away in a box in my storage unit. It's a wonder Pamela even continued speaking to me after that shun. A few months ago, while rummaging through my mountains of yard sale fodder, I unearthed the deck. Something told me to bring them home. So, after a hiatus, they're residing once more on the altar, hopefully collecting more energy than dust.

September 18th of this year marked the 64th anniversary of the passing of Pamela Coleman Smith. I wanted to post something on my Facebook page about her. So, I simply did some snooping on line and found an intriguing illustration that was part of an art exhibit in New York in 1907.

She inscribed it to Alfred Stieglitz, the owner of the museum where her exhibit was held. She wrote:

"To one who appreciates what this means."
With good wishes from Pamela Coleman Smith.
January 24, 1907.

She wrote it on MY birth date in 1907. It was written 54 years to the day before I was born and I "coincidentally" found it 54 years later. There I am, smack-dab in the middle of things. Again, "To one who appreciates what this means." Those words vibrated more deeply within me than a tuning fork in an earthquake. When my peeps want to make their presence known they don't hold back.

A couple of days later, I was preparing to post one of my CARD OF THE DAY messages. I couldn't quite decide which deck to use. I picked up a couple and my energy flat lined. Nothing there. Then I was drawn to the Daily Guidance from your Angels Oracle Deck. I shuffled for quite awhile. Finally, a card flew out…

"PERFECT TIMING. Now is the perfect moment for you to act on your inspirations. The doors are open, while you walk through them with us by your side. Don't delay or procrastinate, as all of the ingredients are ripe for your success. Everything and everyone is on your side, supporting your positive outcome."

That resonated strongly within me and, by the response to it, several felt the same way. Excellent! Time to clock out early and grab a Corona! Of course, it didn't quite go that way. It never does.

Craig, a friend in Florida, emailed me:

"Okay, so I pulled a card, too. Just because you did. MOM, CRAIG IS COPYING ME AGAIN! (Note: You can clearly see why we get along)

"The Six of Wands. Generally speaking, when the Six of Wands appears in a reading, the querent will find that obstacles will be overcome with ease and advancement in their life will occur quickly. They seem blessed at this time, with people praising them and offering them golden opportunities.

"This reminds us that when we believe in ourselves and have confidence in our own abilities and character, we have already won the hardest part of the battle."

The message goes hand in hand with the Oracle Card I had drawn as well as what is going on within my own life at the moment. Once I saw his email I was "told" to draw a card from MY Rider-Waite deck. Again, I have not touched this deck in YEARS. That deck was boxed up when I left Arizona in 2009, untouched and nearly forgotten. So, I pushed Pamela's picture aside, blew dust off the box (my maid hasn't shown up to work since I politely pointed out the fact that she just doesn't exist) and opened it. I slid the deck out of its cardboard packaging and into the palm of my hand. Care to take a guess as to what card was facing me when I slipped the deck out of the box?

The real kicker? I'm a Six in Numerology.

Then IT happened. My beloved cohort, my partner in crime, my twin from another mother popped in for a visit: DOUBT. Seriously, people, what is wrong with me? If They club me over the head any harder my dome will pop like a ripe gourd on a hot summer day. (My apologies if you happen to be eating right now) Whenever I teach I always pound TRUST into the brains of my students. I all but beat them with the word. (Hurt me, beat me, teach me trust!) Trust what you get, what you feel, what you hear and sense. Then I turn around and pull this stupid stunt?

"Idiot."
Michelle

I can talk myself out of nearly anything. It's a gift, really. A useless one, like an alarm clock for an insomniac, but a gift just the same. I can easily accept the many amazing experiences of other people. But, when it comes to my own, I have to chew that jerky just a little too much, beat that dead horse long after its drawn its final breath. I actually spent more time than I'm willing to admit trying to convince myself that the chances of two people across the country from one another drawing the exact same card is an hourly occurrence. Keep in mind I consider watching reruns of The Love Boat to be quality time so I'm not much of a gauge. My favorite expressions with my Guides seem to be, "This can't be real" and "What does all of this mean?"

My Guides have a couple favorite expressions for me, too. But it contains far too many expletives to share here.

On my way home from running errands the next morning, all snugly wrapped up in my big, ol' burrito of doubt, a car zipped out in front of me as if driven by Speed Racer. Once the driver secured his place at the head of the line, he then felt compelled to drive at a speed that can only be represented as a negative number. I'm grumbling the whole time, of course. We were coasting along through the streets of Long Beach at a rate that would make The Poky Little Puppy seem like The Flash. As I shot death rays out of my eyes, I realized the car had a vanity tag. I had to blink a time or two in disbelief as my jaw began swaying in the breeze.

"Holy—" was all I managed to say before I burst out laughing. Staring back at me from the back-end of a car—in big, bold, DMV lettering—was a license plate boasting the name, 'PAMIE C'. Whenever I'm pissed at Pamela I always call her "Pamie." And "C"… well, that's so self-explanatory that even I get it. Once the realization slapped the doubt outta me, the damn car sped up. "Oh, that's just great!" I screamed to no one in particular. "He decides to run amok NOW?" I chased it down, like a deranged stalker, in order to snap a quick shot. The car went off in a different direction at the very next intersection after I took the picture. I have to admit I don't blame the guy. If I saw a man in my rearview mirror laughing like a maniac and snapping pictures, I'd drive like a bat outta hell, too.

Keep that little tidbit in mind the next time you're stuck behind a slow driver.

It looks like I need to rethink my expressions. 'This can't be real' has become, 'This IS real.' As to what it all means… well, that's the juicy one. It means several things. First of all, it means I need to practice what I preach and teach: TRUST. My Guides always let me know they are there, working in the background, just doing what they do. I know they are—I can feel them—but the physical reminders are always the ones that truly blow me away. It's the same for you, you know? Trust that your Guides are right there, by your side, supporting you at every turn. You don't really need to know their names. I know, in my heart of hearts, that the names they give me are just to appease my silly mortal mind. Call them what you will. If a name pops into your head out of allegedly nowhere, then go with it. Or just call 'em, 'Hey, You!' They'll still answer.

You must understand that they cannot make your decisions for you. We're here living a physical life for a variety of reasons. Actually living that life is in the forefront. We make choices and we live through them the best we can. For example, I choose to be a blockhead. I do that of my own free to reasonably priced will. But my Entourage continues strengthening Their connection with me and They do their best to chisel away at my cement-lined stubbornness…and thank God they do. Thanks to Them, I have been blessed to be a part of something for the past 14 years that can only be described as miraculous.

What is Pamela up to? What message is she sending me? I honestly do not know. First and foremost, she is making her presence and participation in my life blatantly obvious. Perhaps my wanting to bring attention to her namesake on the anniversary of her passing brought it all on. Or maybe I was supposed to honor Miss Smith in my own way so Pamela could wave me down with her semaphore flags. The chicken or the egg? Who knows? I have to TRUST that it's OK that I do not know. There's always a reason. Always. So, again, what does all of this mean? It also means that despite my faults and flaws, my peeps won't give up on me, my destiny, my path, my work... my very being. If THEY aren't about to give up on me then it would be rude if I did not return the favor. I will simply continue through the clouded confusion of, as the Guide of a client of mine says, 'this glorious life.'

Want a good laugh? PAMIE C, in Numerology, is an 11. A big "thumbs up" from my Guides.

Thank you, Pamela, may I have another?

"You cannot take the hand of another without extending yours as well. In order to be a part of the chain—the link—you must take part in the chain."

Pamela

"Gabriel's Return"

I'VE EASILY READ HUNDREDS OF PEOPLE over my years as a working medium. And, by sheer logic, I've connected with even more spirits. For the most part the souls I've encountered—both of the pulse-steady and pulse-impaired variety—have melted into one colossal blob. It's nothing personal, I assure you. Seriously, do you remember each and every person, upright or not, that you encounter?

I always explain to my sitters that I rarely retain any information brought forth in a reading. It's the difference between telling your own story as opposed to telling the tale of another. You recall the vivid details of your own life but only bits and pieces of the tale of another. Some highlights will stand out along the way. Something that strikes your funny bone, makes your stomach turn or even makes the hair on your neck stand on end, turn white and then fall out. Our lives are the Main Feature while everyone else's is merely a pre-matinee trailer. I bet THAT realization makes you feel so gosh-darn special.

Don't let this worry you. The vast majority of the ones I remember are because it's something really funny, weird or, honestly, just plain stupid. What's that? You want an example? Well, OK, if you insist…

I vividly recall a time when I informed a sitter, "Your father is here."

She immediately jumped in feet first to correct me. "No, he's not!" she exclaimed. "He's dead!"

After a very well-timed pause, I said dryly, "How closely did you read my business card?" Trust me when I tell you she turned a shade of red that I will never forget.

I once connected with a man who passed tragically at only 50. He was engaged and already to start another chapter in his life as a married man. I felt a huge slam in my chest, the sign given to indicate a massive heart attack. I relayed this information to his fiancé. She exclaimed, "Oh, yes, he DID have a heart attack! He was sitting on the toilet and just fell over dead!"

I heard the Spirit say, "Oh, great. You had to tell him THAT, didn't you?" At the end of the session he showed me an innocent looking item—I won't say what—indicating it was something he loved and it meant a lot to him. I was clueless as to what he was really saying. She screamed, "Oh, my GOD! I can't believe he'd bring THAT up!" She was laughing so hard I thought she was going to have her own coronary. The mysterious item in question, while a commonplace thing, is also slang for a very specific sex act. One, I then discovered, was a favorite in his repertoire. As she calmed herself down, her late fiancé said, "That'll teach her to tell people I died taking a crap." I'm not forgetting that one no matter how much I try.

So, as you can see, some stick out in my mind. There are also a few who make quite an impact on me. Not only on my career as a medium, but simply as a human being. They go beyond the call of duty to remind us of the strength of unconditional and unending love.

I have had those in Spirit assist me in readings for individuals they didn't even know in life. They have helped the other spirits make a better connection with me. They have shown up to serve as an example of what another soul was truly about in their own life. In essence, I help them and they help me. And, of course, all connections originate from one place and for one purpose: Love.

Out of all of the Spirits I have happily encountered, I have to say that a man by the name of Gabriel has claimed a secure spot in the top five. Look up "determination" in Webster's and you will likely find "See Gabriel" as the singular definition.

I first encountered Gabriel on a flight to Wisconsin in 2014. He literally stalked me across half the country, making his presence unmistakable time and time again. He kept piling it on until I finally found myself with his fiancé, Danielle, and her mother at one of my group demonstrations. I wrote about it all so others could absorb the experience and his powerful message.

I am often directed by Spirit to purchase small trinkets and bring them to my group demonstrations. I never know who will receive the item. It is soul-ly up to "them". I'm Spirit's Vanna White. They turn on the light and I just reveal the letter. Fortunately, Spirit makes this very affordable by leading me to area Thrift Shops or homes of vacationing families who don't bother turning on their security systems. They send me off on these little scavenger hunts in my hometown as well as cities and centers where I am traveling. I merely walk into the brick and mortar building and wander around until something strikes me. I am not sure how I know what to pick up. I can't describe it any better than saying, "I just know." I don't get anything clairsentiently or clairvoyantly. It's a feeling of all knowing that I personally refer to as "Clair-YuhHuh."

My annual trek to Wisconsin has made me quite familiar with the Dime and Dollar Thrift Store, a fun little shop in Stevens Point. I know the lay of the land quite well now. If my cast-in-stone routine was any more predictable, the world would use it, and not the sun, to check their clocks. My normal route takes me through the glass door and passed the display case doubling as a checkout counter on the right. My first stop is a rack of bric-a-brac on the left. I circle it with the same dogged determination as I hover over a bin of chocolate pudding at any semi-respectful buffet. Something will just grab my attention and I grab it in return. It's almost as if it flashes at me, like one of those Instamatic Camera Cubes from the 70's. I then circle off to the right to graze through any CD's that have, for any range of reasons, found themselves there. Retreating to the back room, I swoop down on every book I can find strewn over a span of several mismatched bookshelves. Then I flip through a bin of LP's just so I can feel really old. A walk on the wild geriatric side will bring you right back to earth whenever you're feeling exceptionally good about yourself.

With the Bay City Rollers echoing in my head, I will meander through small electronics and kitchen accessories. Then I wrap everything up looking through a hodgepodge of tumblers and coffee mugs. I see everything from #1 TEACHER to DOLLYWOOD OR BUST spewing before me like a marquee on crack. I will then take my haul, no more than 2 or 3 items, and amble my way back to the checkout counter. A couple bucks later and I'm the temporary caretaker of the bounty until each is passed on to the intended recipient.

My latest sparing shopping spree, however, paid no attention to my well-crafted routine. Upon entering, I made an immediate sharp left and found myself immersed in a jungle of book bags, clothing and doilies. I was in foreign territory. Clothing? Really? If you know me then you know my sense of fashion makes no sense. I own two pairs of shoes for crying out loud. TWO. And I cannot, for the life of me, fathom why anyone would EVER need a third. I buy a pair of sneakers. I wear them every day so they last about a year and a few months. When they show their signs of wear-and-tear, I buy an identical pair to replace them. I own four denim long-sleeve shirts. They're identical. Variety is not in my spice rack, lemme tell ya.

So, completely out of my element, wondering if I need a passport, I took a 360 degree view of my surroundings. I figured I was there for a reason so off I trudged into the sea of racks and hangers. Turning a corner, I spied a backpack on the floor leaning against a chrome set of shelves. This grabbed my attention because my own needs replacing. I picked it up and gave it a once-over. I placed it back on the floor while making a mental note to ponder the purchase prior to my departure.

I returned to my traditional pathway and, indeed, was lead to two items along the way. Remaining true to myself, I sought out the backpack once more. I placed my soon to be purchased items on a shelf in front of me, paying no attention to its contents, and turned my focus on the backpack once more. I picked it up and inspected it with more scrutiny. The bubble of my initial inspection burst with a deafening dose of disappointment within a few seconds. Holes, frayed straps and a cracked coating joined in a rousing harmonious chorus of the "Don't Buy 'Dis, Dufus" Boogie.

I shrugged as I bent down to return it to the floor once again. In mid-bend I glanced up to see a stack of well-worn satchels staring me down. I dropped the backpack as my jaw fell open. My eyes widened as I remained frozen in the hunched over position. I then uttered the only thing an enlightened sort like myself can in a moment like this... "Well, son of a bitch." Emblazoned in black marker across the side of a bag was the name GABRIEL. I straightened up and just laughed aloud. Of all the bags in the stack of 10 or more, only ONE had a name written on it.

I knew Danielle was planning to attend my second group demo the next evening. I loved the fact that I already had a story for her. Sometimes Spirit just makes my job all the easier with stunts like this! I snapped a photo of the bag as I said, "Thanks, Gabe!" I then retrieved my other items from the shelf above my head. It was only then that I realized that I had placed them on top of a large crystal dish. Not just any dish, you know? It was in the shape of a heart. I picked it up and gazed into it, slack jawed. Then I heard Gabe say, in a most serious tone, "Give it to her with my love and my blessing."

I shook my head in wonder. No matter how many times I experience moments like this, I am always blown away. There's nothing routine about this! I nodded and said, "You got it, dude." My California Surfer Guide sneaks out from time to time…

I take my responsibility to Spirit very seriously. Unlike many mediums, however, I manage to have a lot of fun with it. I gave Gabriel my word and that IS my bond. If my tongue happens to be firmly planted in my cheek while I carry out my welcomed obligation, then so be it. (Cue diabolical twirling of my mustache) Little did I know at the time, but I was going to have to really work a bit to pull this one off. I hate when They make me sweat.

Saturday came and went. The sold out demo was a rousing success. An evening of both healing laughter and tears brought everyone together. There was only one little hiccup in this otherwise perfect evening: Danielle was a no-show. I was quite perplexed, as was Gabriel, I'm sure. Danielle's punctuality was never questioned. If she said she was going to be there, she was going to be there. She may burst through the door at the last second but, by Golly, she was THERE. But not this time. Once I returned to my lodging, I emailed her just to ensure all was well. The email went unanswered. So, I lugged her heart to my next group demonstration. Again, she didn't show up. I drove to my home away from home, entered my room and was immediately greeted by Gabriel's tell-tale cigarette smoke. "Dude," I said aloud, "Get her here! I don't know what to do!" The smoke dissipated and I finally calmed myself enough to catch some Z's.

I took a couple of days off from my rigorous schedule to visit a dear (live) friend near Chicago. While there, I received an email from Danielle. Way to go, Gabe! Something came up at the last minute and she was unable to attend. She asked for info on my other appearances and events. She assured me that she would attend one of them.

Again, she was as visible as Big Foot. And, yes, I found myself accosted by cigarette smoke. Oh, joy. The dead are, if anything, determined…and dead. After my final group gathering, on November 3, I sent her a text asking if she could meet me for breakfast the next morning. I told her I only had one day left in town and it was imperative that I see her. I didn't tell her, but I really didn't want to continue my journey with this Pig-Pen cloud of smoke hovering over me the whole time. She promptly agreed to our getting together over syrup and powdered sugar at ten the next morning. I had reached the end of my patience with Gabriel's second-world-second-hand smoke. I guess you can say I just couldn't HACK it.

Ahem.

I snagged a table in the back of the South Point Restaurant. I love this local diner. You get a gluttonous mound of food nearly obliterating your plate from view for a price that makes you look for the Fonz in the corner. They've also dedicated an entire wall to the miracle of bacon. I'm on board with anyone who worships Meat Candy.

Danielle dashed in with her twinkling eyes and a smile that can make you forget ANYTHING has ever been wrong in this, or any, life. After a hug and a laugh, we scanned the menus and placed our orders (both of which would piss off any cardiologist worth their weight in lard). Once the formalities were cast aside, and I knew we wouldn't be interrupted by a waitress hell-bent on refilling any and all containers on our table, I proceeded to the heart of the matter. I ran through the whole story. My trek to the Dime and Dollar, my diverted route inside, the backpack. Everything. Her doe-like eyes widened even more when I showed her the photo of Gabriel's bag (I honestly didn't think they COULD get any wider!). Then I saw the very same windows of her soul glisten slightly when I handed her the crystal heart. I didn't permit my gaze to linger beyond a cursory glance. That was their moment, just between them.

She sat there, looking at it, running her fingers around the edge, retracing the shape in her own heart. Then she smiled. She looked up at me and said, "You have NO idea what this means." She nodded her head slightly. "You see, I collect cut crystal exactly like this. And, in my whole collection, I don't have anything like this one." She held it up with her right hand and waved it slightly. "I understand the message, too. His telling me he gives his blessing...you see, I met someone. I met him ON Valentine's Day." She smiled again. "I've always said I knew Gabe sent him to me. It ALL makes sense." She returned her smiling eyes to the crystal heart and, for a moment, to Gabriel. And I haven't smelled his smoke since.

Again, we don't die. And, logic tells us, that if WE don't die then our love certainly can't, either. For whatever reason, Gabriel chose me. He sought me out and entrusted me, of all people, to help him help his lady love. He has an open-door policy with me. This sort of access is my equivalent of joining the Five-Timer's Club on SNL. He has joined the ranks of other Spirits that I hold near and dear. I've never met any of them in the physical but I sure feel like I know them now. Gabriel is now hobnobbing with Jason, Alex, David and, my forever #1 gal, Dana. They have all allowed me to observe such perfect examples of unending love and I am grateful beyond words. And I cannot think of a better time to acknowledge that gratitude as Thanksgiving approaches.

Take a moment to acknowledge the loves in your life, both here and there. They never leave us. As long as there is love there is that eternal connection. Send them your prayers, your gratitude, your hugs, your laughter, your high-fives. Express it in any way you want and it IS received with open arms and crystal hearts.

It's an honor, Gabe. Truly an honor. And I thank you.

"Playing with Mediumship"

HAVING GROWN UP AS AN ONLY CHILD, my so-called social life consisted of mingling and hobnobbing my toys. As any only child will attest, you are always on a constant search for new-fangled ways to entertain yourself. Personally, I became very adept at playing most board games as a lone player. I could objectively play games of chess, Monopoly, Life—even Sorry—against myself. I've always had a strong love of board games simply because they involve two of my favorite pastimes: concentrating and sitting. Sitting is underrated. It really is. Die-hard sitting takes commitment and determination. Ask anyone with ADHD. One day I will have a pillow embroidered with these soulful words:

> *"If It Shan't Be Done Whilst Sitting*
> *Then 'Tis Not Worth Doing!"*

Despite my adoration of those geniuses at Milton Bradley, my favorite toy of all time was my odds-and-ends assortment of various plastic figures. I had accumulated, over time and by no intended purpose, a green draw-string bag filled to the brim with an ill-fitted bevy of cowboys, Indians, astronauts, soldiers and even Presidents. Yes, you read that correctly. I had John Adams and Abe Lincoln in full living color and a plain white Dwight Eisenhower (accurately depicted, I do believe). They stood approximately 2 ½" in height. I have no vivid recollection of how they came to be a part of my collection. They were just always there. Eisenhower's head was lopsided because, early on, I discovered that I could write on the sidewalk using his Presidential cranium like a piece of chalk. Clearly, I did not like Ike.

I would spend long hours, day after day, immersed in the world I created with my plastic playmates. Each one had a name and a very specific role in our world. There was a band of heroes led by The Professor (an old west doctor holding a medical bag). He was assisted by Alex and Jane (both being Native American figures, red and blue respectively) and Hans (a confederate soldier separated from his regiment when he was caught up in the aftermath of a time machine the Professor had invented—who hasn't had THAT happen at some point?). A reoccurring character was a Viking named Thor (I pride myself on the originality of names). He was another victim of one of the Professor's time machine mishaps. Later plots revealed that Thor and Hans had actually been brothers in a previous life. They fought various Batman-Inspired villains such as The Evil Bozo (where DO I come up with these brilliant names anyway?). He was a bendable Gumby-Like Bozo the Clown who had his arms torn off in some freak undisclosed accident. This once beloved circus clown was now engulfed by his hatred of the world. Quite the diabolical mastermind, lemme tell ya.

The point? Each and every one of them was as real as any flesh and blood person in my life. I could retreat myself into them and their plane of reality effortlessly. Some would say that action was a defense mechanism, that I was hiding from something and ignoring reality. I'm sure there is some truth to that notion—what 7 year old doesn't get their reality and imagination mixed together? Looking back through my trusty Hind-Sight X-Ray Specs, I can "see" how my frolicking imagination was preparing me for my future, both at the drawing board and on the platform.

First is the unfaltering believability of it all. I didn't think my toys were alive and real. I KNEW it. There wasn't a doubt in my little, open mind of this. Do you remember your favorite childhood toy? Your doll, teddy bear or train were each a part of your posse. They were your peeps! They had your back! How many of us curled up with our favorite stuffed animal at night KNOWING we would be safe as we slumbered? Our toys were really our first experiences in having faith, the all-knowing sense that it "is".

Second is the open unobstructed dialogue. I did not just talk FOR my toys, I talked TO them. They heard me and would speak with me in return. The Professor and crew had their own distinct voices and personalities so I could easily tell one from another. I knew how each would react to any given situation. I knew their strong points and weaknesses. I definitely knew one from another.

Finally, I would merely allow the adventure to unfold before me in whatever way it needed. I gave up control of the moment and allowed it to just be what it is. This simple act enables the enjoyment while eradicating the expectations. I discovered that relinquishing control is liberating. Quite the statement for an adult diagnosed as an Early On-Set Control Freak.

In cartooning, my truest love, I have to believe in the characters that I draw. In order for them to make sense to the reader, they MUST make sense to me. They. Are. Real. Then comes the dialogue between creator and character, then character to character, and ultimately character to reader. But, in order for the reader to "hear" them, the initial connection from the creator is an absolute must. In the end I simply let the cartoon draw itself. I may have an initial idea of where it SHOULD be going but, more times than not, I find it going in some other direction. The work always speaks loudly and comfortably on its very own when I allow that to happen.

Nearly verbatim, the same philosophies can be said about mediumship. I truly KNOW the connection is real. I trust The Creator and the connection within. Those in Spirit are as much alive as my toys of yore and my current creations sprawled crossways over Bristol. Once that initial realization is embraced, I latch myself onto the dialogue. Whether it is between me and a Spirit Guide or a "Deceased" Loved One, the exchange, in whatever form it is in, is vital. I allow them to speak their minds, their souls, as they "see" fit. And, finally, I just toss up my hands and do my best to release the control to "Upper Management". I watch AND listen as it is merely played out.

A trail of breadcrumbs is sprinkled before us from the onset. There are times when the path is crystal freakin' clear—but rarely. Most of the time it's a blissful blur of wonder and (alleged) confusion. However, on those cool summer nights of reflection we are given the reward of reasoning. Out of the blue it suddenly makes sense. We finally find the reason 'why' dancing right in front of us in a well-choreographed Busby Berkley Extravaganza. "Now I understand," you'll say as a smile of knowing, of faith, spreads across your lips.

Make a point, when that AH-HA Moment strikes, to offer your appreciation to all parties involved. The medium and the cartoonist in me are certainly grateful to that imaginative little boy from ~~not~~ so long ago. His daring diversions cast a firm foundation through his misinterpreted monkey business. Through his unplanned playing, I was led to a life of wonder, joy and continual healing laughter. It is misunderstood by some but it has never been, nor will it ever be, misGUIDEd.

"Speak It, Teach It"

I ACTUALLY HELM A WEEKLY MEDIUMSHIP DEVELOPMENT CIRCLE every Sunday in Signal Hill. Some of you are, in all probability, scratching your head over this one. If you know me, you also know that teaching is not one of my favorite pastimes. Teaching ranks right down there with holiday family dinners, raisins and Country Caterwauling that some insist is music. I've always assumed my dislike for teaching stems from my lifelong loathing of school in general. I often feel like the character in the Far Side cartoon asking his teacher, "Mr. Osborne, may I be excused? My brain is full." I was bored to tears the vast majority of the time back in my school days. And it wasn't because I was some unearthly genius, either. Good heavens, no. I just resented anyone telling me what to do. (A delightful quirk that I clutch onto with a stubborn death grip to this very day.) Even then I knew the path my life would be taking. I was going to be a cartoonist and that journey would not involve algebra or geometry. I guess you could say, upon reflection, that little snippet was one of my earliest psychic predictions. Move over, Madam Olga, there's a new Criswell on the block.

So, why on earth (or any other plane of existence you prefer) did I decide to take on this class? That's a damn fine question. Honestly, I did it out of sheer boredom. I was looking to shake things up, do something different, so I put that desire out there to my Guides. When will I ever learn? Once again, Robert and the Gang opted to take me at my word and toss me in head first. Way to go, Guys (and Gals). The class had originally been taught by someone else, but he moved out of the area. A couple of his students came to me and asked if I would be interested in stepping in as their new teacher. Great Googly

Moogly, what were they thinking? SERIOUSLY? That's like putting me in charge of the dessert cart. You just know nothing good is gonna come out of it.

When I teach, I like to push the envelope, test new ideas, take students down unfamiliar pathways. It's fun to dive into the deep end of the pool without an inflatable clown-character raft.

Not knowing what will happen is a great spiritual aphrodisiac.

My personal theory is that your connection with your own Spirit Guides is singularly the most important aspect of this work. The stronger the communication, the personal connection, the clearer the corridor. This connection can take you to uncharted places with unbridled passion. The more I discover, the more I want to know. The more I know, the more I want to share with anyone within a somewhat interested earshot. I'm not one for rambling lectures. The learning—the excitement—is in the actual doing, not in the humdrum listening and waiting.

So, to keep things lively, I've opened the door to channeling for my band of students. I've shown them exercises in meeting with their Spirit Guides—hobnobbing with them if you will—and even their Higher Selves. I've taken them to the next stage of conversing with them through Automatic Writing (a true passion for me). Channeling seemed like the logical next step along the way. This builds trust as well as comfort in your connection to your Spiritual Peeps, your Crew. I assure you that channeling is NOT for everyone. But it will allow you to better feel, and understand, the energy of your own Guides. This comes in especially handy for those times when you think, "I can't feel my Guides around me! Where are they?" We all do it from time to time. Trust me on this. You will, by merely raising your own sensitivity and awareness, find that statement will all but completely vanish from your daily diatribe. And how cool would THAT be?

I know what you're saying… "Hey, Charles, it sure sounds like you're teaching right now!" Yeah, whatEVER. I'm doing it while nibbling on a cold frosted strawberry Pop-Tart and sipping an ice-cold glass of milk. I can deal with that.

The class had some major breakthroughs this past week. I was extremely proud of my students and their accomplishments (Pop-Tarts would have improved the experience but, hey, you can't have everything). Some very intense messages, emotionally as well as philosophically, came through each student. There's nothing like a good dose of self awareness to wake you up in the middle of the afternoon. Normally, I will go into channel first in order to set the tone of the exercise. It is also good for students who have never experienced anything like this to see a bit of the possibilities lying ahead for them. Last week, however, I was told in no uncertain terms, I had to wait until the end. While unhappy about being told what to do, I begrudgingly admitted that They are always right. Just like my editor, but I digress… So, like a good whipping boy, I waited.

When I channel, privately or in public demonstrations, I discover there is a protocol. Robert always opens and closes the session. He has a ritual that he has gone through since day one. Then he will move onto whatever topic he deems necessary for those in attendance. Once he takes care of his agenda others may, from time to time, pop in for more commentary. It is interesting to hear the view points of the others. They merely offer their take, their spin, on Robert's initial message. Once they are finished Robert will pop back in with a quick summation or message and then off they go.

Robert, and Robert alone, always opens the floor for a Q&A when I am giving a public channeling demonstration. He doesn't bother with personal questions ("Should I move to another town," etc). He is looking for questions of a Universal, a more spiritual, nature. "If you broaden your mind you will surely enhance your intentions," Robert says, "Imagine the possibilities within THAT!" The ONLY time this protocol was broken was during a demo at a New Age Center in Fullerton, CA, a few years ago. Robert had taken a couple of inquiries from those in attendance, as is his custom. Then one woman asked a question and, much to everyone's surprise, Robert stepped aside and allowed Dondi to speak! This was the first and, as of this date, the only time that has occurred.

A little background on Dondi. He is a three-dimensional version of the comic strip character by Irwin Hasen. He is about 5 years of age. His love of life is contagious. It's really fitting because I am a cartoonist, as you know, AND I'm an adoptee. The whole package is once again wrapped up neatly and beautifully. Realizing that my Joy Guide is a 5 year old REALLY explains a lot about me, doesn't it?

Dondi answered her question and then Robert returned to continue. I later discovered that the woman who asked the question had a daughter whose name is Dondi AND she was named after the comic strip character! So, once again, proof that the interaction is never random. There's always a reason. ALWAYS. We may not get it at the time but, trust me, one day it will all come together.

You're wondering what Robert had to say this past Sunday, aren't you? Well, speculate no more, for here are Their words. Happy mulling!

ROBERT

"Lovely to see you. More lovely to see your experiences today. Intoxicating, isn't it? This is to be understandable. For some, it is very new. And, with the newness, comes intensity, fascination, sadness. But not [sadness] in a sorrowful way. Perhaps a sadness of what you may have missed by not pursuing this communiqué sooner. A sadness for missing emotion of the heart. Sadness of not really believing… not mentioning any names. (*Whispers*) Is Kevin listening? (*loudly*) HAHA!

[FYI: Kevin and I are both life-long members of The Bull-Headed Skeptics Club. We have a secret handshake and everything.]

"Your ways are not foreign to us [Kevin]. If you had to work with this (*pointing to self*) you would understand. HAHA! It is true. He HAS driven me to drink. HAHA!

"Right now, the levity felt in your hearts, in your consciousness… do you feel that? (*Snaps fingers 5 times*) The guards come down so you may see. And what you see, my friends, is but merely the beginning. If you never do this again you will always have this experience. But, since you have touched it, taken it, you want to try it again, don't you? Again… *intoxicating*. Allow the excitement, the wonder, the curiosity to lead you, entice you and, most importantly, BE you.

"Your soul craves the connection of 'home'. The body knows it is home but you understand, now, the duality. What you see is not always what you get. For what you are seeing is always a little more complicated. Look beyond what SEEMS in order to see what IS."

PAMELA

"Oh, he's not going to be happy that I'm here. (*Long sigh, as if exhaling smoke*)

"Hello, my friends. I… am… Pamela. I am, as my host would say, a bit of a smart ass. But would you expect anything else? (*Whispers*) I don't think so.

"Robert speaks of what is seen, what is felt, what is processed (*she pronounced it as PRO-cessed*). *I* understand the individual versions of what your eyes, what your mind, tells you. Rebeka, Love, first word that comes to your mind when I say the word, 'Radio'?"

Rebeka: *Frequency*.

"Shawn… same question."

Shawn: *Transmission*.

"Two different answers! Which is correct? Both! 'Frequency' for Rebeka, 'Transmission' for Shawn. Each of you has a set of, shall we say, encyclopedias in one's mind, in one's heart. Rely on these. *Rely on these.*

"One continually asks for a sign. We are not in the billboard business! But… but… beyond the billboards you seek—or THINK you should see—that is where the signs ARE. That is where the signs are. If you do not understand what you are feeling, focus on what you are seeing. How does THAT make you FEEL? And your answers can be there. It will not always be black and white. WHY? Because you have to work through it. THROUGH IT.

"Why? Why not? Think about that. WHY NOT? To desire knowledge, to crave knowledge, you must first dive into it. Play with it. And let it be whatever it needs to be for you. Each of you."

ROBERT

"I am Robert. With our collective hearts, our collective thoughts, our collective intentions, and, of course, our collective love, you are thanked, you are appreciated. And, until next time, I am done."

With those three little words—I AM DONE—Robert was "gone". I know he wasn't truly gone but his focus, his energy, was hurled back from hence it came. I always feel an odd emptiness when he has stepped back. I mean I'm plugged into this intense generator when, all of a sudden, the power source is shut off faster than he can snap my fingers. What never ceases to amaze me is the depth of Their brevity. The messages are always deceivingly short. But, if you re-read them, over and over, you'll discover such complexity and influence within the few sentences that have been given. I'm always left in a state of awe. I know my own words. I know the pattern and rhythm of my own speech. I stare at the messages given and my first thought is always, "That is NOT me!"

If They can provide words through me that are not my own, then they can just as easily push, poke and prod me into other things that are not necessarily my own preferred actions, such as teaching. It isn't fully me at the podium. I know that. But, if I truly did not want to teach, I would not be doing it (as much as I hate to admit it). I have had, from the onset, this simple philosophy regarding mediumship: I will quit the instant it stops being fun. The same can be said about teaching, too, I suppose. I like to push my students out of their comfort zone because I know they'll learn from the experience. My Guides enjoy doing the exact same thing to me. What a friggin' shock.

The lesson here? You need to embrace each and every part of yourself. The dark and the light, the cozy and the discomfort, the chocolate and the broccoli. It's all there for a reason. As Pamela asked, "How does THAT make you FEEL?" Mull it over, kids. Class dismissed.

"Heaven's Kitchen"

I'VE BEEN TRYING TO COME UP WITH A WAY to describe our dad. My mind reels at the wide array of adjectives swirling through my head. Do you know what I've discovered? It's not an easy task to just "sum up a person." Summarizing our dad is like saying the Himalayas are just a couple of hills. When I was a kid, Reader's Digest—the IDEAL publication for those with ADHD—ran a regular feature entitled, ***"The Most Unforgettable Person I Ever Met."*** Well, let me tell you, if Everett Kitchen is ANYTHING, it is 'unforgettable.' His warmth is an inferno. His generosity extends beyond a vanishing point on the far horizon. I could go on and on about his loyalty, his genuine heart, his devotion to family and friends, his sense of humor. All of the traits that we already know so well, and are already missing.

There are several things I will miss, of course. His hugs, for example. He would just engulf you in those massive arms of his. You'd struggle, but only in jest. Once there, you just didn't want to leave because you were home. Another thing is his "seal of approval." I'm sure we've all heard it at one point or another.

Someone would ask, "Hey, Kitch, how's that bowl of chili?"

He'd answer excitedly, *"Woot! I mean to tell ya!"*

"Isn't that funny, Kitch?"

"Woot! I mean to tell ya!"

He is his own man with his own style.

His surname couldn't be any more appropriate. Seriously, what that man could do in a kitchen was something wedged between a miracle and a masterpiece. A stove and a spatula were his brushes while an empty plate and stomach were his canvases. If you know me then you know I'm quite the accomplished art collector… He did everything in his power to make sure no one left his home hungry. And, if he went to YOUR place, he'd bring the food to you or make it there himself. And, if by some freak of nature, you DID go away hungry… well, it was your own damn fault.

Kitch brought a lot to the table, both literally and figuratively. Whether it is the dinner table or to whatever relationship you had with him. Parent. Family. Friend. Co-worker. Partner in Crime. It didn't matter because any table setting with him was as beautiful as it was memorable. It overflowed with all and more than you needed, let alone expected. And, if by some random hiccup in the Universe, you couldn't find what you wanted, then he'd find a way to get it for you.

He was a father and an unconventional one at that. He didn't raise us as a traditional Ward Cleaver sort. But his love for all of us was never hidden or denied. He bubbled over with love and pride for his kids. He was always willing to offer a helping hand, a kind word, a flick on the back of the head if we'd wander too far off the expected path. He gave us room to breathe, to falter, to experience life as WE saw it and to learn from our successes as well as our failures. He always encouraged each of us to stand and evolve on our own, and that included falling as well. He graciously and generously offered advice, encouragement, and unending love. He also had absolutely no problem serving up his completely unedited opinions. His views, like his love, were given freely, without hesitation or reserve, whether you wanted it or not. If you asked him a question you'd better be willing to hear the answer!

I am an adoptee. My birth mother was not in a position to care for me properly. She felt I would have a better chance if she put me up for adoption. My mom who raised me, who is a hair shy of 93 and feisty as ever, has always been upfront with me about my adoption. She was very supportive when I began my search for my biological families—my roots—over 30 years ago (By the way, I began my search when I was 8…). I was 33 years old when I spoke to Everett the very first time. I first spoke to my birth-mother three weeks earlier. I was welcomed by her, and her family, with open arms. However, I honestly believed I would NOT have a relationship with my birth-father. I expected to be denied and turned away. In my experiences, birth fathers are more likely to shun the whole idea while birth mother's are pretty much the opposite. I had a great reunion with my birth mother so I certainly did not expect lightening to strike twice.

Kitch proved to be the wild card. Lightening struck with a blinding intensity and started a fire that burns brilliantly to this day and beyond. Way to go, Dad…

The first five minutes of our initial phone conversation were cordial. Friendly, but understandably guarded. I explained I didn't want anything other than some answers, a peek into on my own history. He told me that he would be happy to tell me what he could.

He then asked, "What's your blood type?"

I fully understood why he asked. We did not have the luxury of having Maury Povich exclaiming, "Everett! You ARE the father!"

Well, he asked so, being the naturally born smart-mouth that I am—*thanks, Dad*—I simply replied, "My blood type? Red."

Then we both howled in laughter. This disruption of the sound barrier was immediately met with our abrupt silence. For the first time in my life I heard my laugh echo back at me.

If you know Kitch, you know THE LAUGH. That garish, glass shattering cackle that has been known to make babies cry and land masses shift.

After a moment of silence Kitch said, "This is real, isn't it?"

I merely answered, "Yea. I guess it is."

That ended any discussion of blood type right then and there. Paternity proven through laughter. IN YOUR FACE, MAURY!

So, yes, I have the laugh. My brother, Markis, has the laugh. My sister, Carletta, has THE LAUGH. Hearing this laugh spew upward and outward from someone standing a petite five-foot-four is, honestly, just plain spooky!

I don't mean to stand here and tell you he was perfect. He wasn't and he'd be the first to admit it. He didn't even meander in a suburb of the gated community of perfection. He was bull-headed. The man took stubborn to a height that any accomplished mountain climber would covet. He was a cut of the 'my way or no way' jib.

On my first visit to his home in Colorado, he had the gall to announce to this City Boy, "We get up at 4 o'clock in the morning around here."

I replied, "Good to know. When I get up at 10 be sure you tell me all about it."

See? I got a little more than just his laugh.

If he didn't like something, whether it be a situation or tuna, he'd let you know about it. He wouldn't shirk away from his opinion and he respected anyone who did the same. He shot from the hip and ricochets be damned. He told me, more than once, "I always speak my mind... when I can find it."

He had zero tolerance for anyone who wallowed in their own self-pity. "If you aren't willing to help yourself," he said, "how can you face yourself in the mirror?"

I looked at him and said, "I sold my mirrors. They were defective."

Once again, that laugh echoed in stereo.

He didn't believe in regrets. Instead, he preferred to own up to what was, focus on what is, and look forward to what may be. An eternal optimist wrapped in a tortilla of sarcasm. Again, unforgettable.

He was a giver. He didn't ask for anything other than honesty and love in return. He received so much more joy when giving to another than getting a glamorous holiday gift himself.

Honestly, if I had to sum him up, I'd have to say our father is about laughter. He instilled that in all of us. He is about joy. He is about giving. And, I mean to tell ya, he is about food! Preparing AND eating! He is also about bringing people together. The turnout today surely proves that. He even managed to wrangle his 4 kids together for the very first time. Talk about being a control freak!

His passing has been such a shock to each and every one of us. How someone so full of life—even BIGGER than life—can be gone so quickly is just a mystery. We're all still trying to wrap our minds around referring to him in the past tense. My sister, Carletta, summed it up best a few days ago. She stepped groggily out of her bedroom one morning and said, "Do you know what I was supposed to be doing today?"

"What's that?" I asked.

She simply said, "Not this."

Boy, Sis, ya got that right.

It's only fitting that Dad passed ON April Fool's Day. If anyone would appreciate the humor it that, it would be him. The real kicker for me is that the very next day, April 2nd, marked the 22nd anniversary of the very first time he and I spoke. The first time I ever heard OUR laugh.

Because of my work as a medium, I know that life never truly ends, that we don't really die. We simply move on. With that in mind, someone recently asked me, "Where do you think he is now?" Honestly, this is how I picture it: Dad makes his way through a field of billowing clouds of dry ice like we see in so many Hollywood movies. After walking for awhile he finally sees a glowing light off in the distance. Instinctively, he begins to walk toward it. As he draws near the light he is is immediately greeted by a pack of hyperactive drooling black labs. Amidst the jumping, licking and yelps of excitement, they manage to lead him to this massive set of pearly gates. The gates open effortlessly because they have WD-40 over there. The opening gates resemble what can only be described as large arms reaching out for a loving, long overdue embrace. The kind that he, himself, always gave. As Kitch's brown eyes adjust to the intense bright light emitting from behind the glistening gates, he finds himself standing in His presence.

The Big Guy standing before The Bigger Guy.

Kitch shrugs unassumingly, flashing that crooked smile of his, and simply drawls, "So, did I do OK?"

And God, in whatever form you see Him, in whatever way you believe, gazes lovingly at His returning son, reflecting that same crooked smile that He, Himself, created, and simply exclaims, *"Woot! I mean to tell ya!"*

We love you, Dad.

"FOR THE LAUGH OF ME"

"Life is the ultimate joke and the Dead 'get it'."
Pretentiously Quoting Myself

ON THE AFTERNOON OF AUGUST 2, 2001, I was a blissfully ignorant sack of meat that didn't bother to give a hoot (whole or half) about anything in this world or any other. I was living right smack-dab in the middle of Bliss-Town with a 90210 zip code. Then, later that night, I was drugged, rolled up into a carpet, stuffed in the trunk of an Eldorado and relocated to a place that I was convinced did not even exist. I didn't end up with just egg on my face, but a whole omelet bar with all the fixin's. But, of course, most of you already know that.

As the 15th Anniversary of my Boot to the Head into mediumship looms, I find myself waxing philosophically about it. Not so much the workings of it all or even the ponderings of how I got here. I've done that far too many times over the past decade and a half. Old news, ya know? I find myself focusing on the on-going WHY of it all. Specifically, WHY do I do what I do? Talking to the Dead: what kind of person decides to do this sort of crazy thing? I assure you Madam Olga was never a Career Day participant when I was in high school. One day you're just sitting there, chatting with Great Uncle Hugh, and then he just keels over. Anyone else would assume the dialogue would end as quickly as he did. But not me. Noooo way. I just continue our conversation despite the fact that most assume Hugh was no longer in a position to be much of a conversationalist. Diving into discussions with the dearly departed does have its downside, lemme tell ya.

I suppose you can say the initial seeds were planted in the very beginning. Since childhood I have had an intense interest in death. No great news flash there. Some would probably term it as an "obsession." While I can understand this judgment call, I am honestly not sure about the accuracy of it. One man's obsession is another man's Sunday afternoon. Admittedly, I've blurred the line separating "interest" and "obsession" so much that the Hubble would have difficulty getting it in focus.

My revered love of cemeteries is my go-to example of this fascination. I'm intrigued how individuals handle death. I've always wondered whose idea it was to dress the deceased in their "Sunday Best" and then throw a huge party for them on the one day their absence is an absolute guarantee. Why do people tend to whisper in funeral homes? It's not like they're gonna wake anyone up. It really makes me happy to see so many are turning away from the traditionally solemn funeral and embracing the idea of a true Celebration of Life. I love how some will include personal items in and around the casket or urn. No pun intended, but it does seem to bring the person to life. For example, my niece slipped a bottle of Pepsi into my birth mother's coffin. My birth father's box of ashes was crowned with a stylish pair of Minnie Mouse ears with DA-DA stitched on the back. Leigh was buried clasping a lapel pin emblazoned with the Bastard Nation logo. I like to envision some yet unborn archeologist of the distant future stumbling upon her crypt one day. The archeologist, upon unsealing it, will exclaim, "Now, THERE is one proud Bastard Goddess!"

Memorials, I feel, should be made more personal. Do not rely on some cookie-cutter format with an "Insert Name Here" approach. I feel the same way about grieving. Death and grieving are very personal things and they should be treated, and respected, as such. Everyone handles them differently. Some linger and dwell while others boldly, while some think coldly, move forward. Mourning isn't a race, people. We're all going at our own pace. My readings over the years have taken on a life of their own (puns are just falling like rain, aren't they?). They are, for the most part, made distinctive by the personal enhancements from Spirit. So, yea, it all tends to tie in together.

There's no doubt about it… I've always found the whole kit n' caboodle pretty interesting. Not necessarily dinner-conversation interesting for most, but interesting just the same. I excitedly discovered, when my birth father passed, that I actually have a cousin who is a mortician. How remarkable is THAT? You have no idea how I wish someone would instate an annual "Take Your Cousin to Work Day."

Cousin Fred makes 'em up while I chat 'em up. That's a sit-com just screaming to happen, folks.

Our presents and futures are always affected by our pasts. The more you analyze your own the more you will uncover. Seemingly random recollections can, one day, bring forth a great epiphany. Attending my great grandmother's funeral, when I was barely 2 years of age, stands out as one of my earliest memories. I can't say I understood on a conscious level, but I assume there was a familiarity on a more subconscious one. Over the years I've heard how many commented on my being so well behaved during the funeral. I've been told I just sat on my mother's lap, looking around with quiet curiosity. Things have changed, of course. I no longer behave OR sit on anyone's lap. One would need major medical for the latter.

I have honestly met many-a-relative 'round a casket—if not IN one—over the years. As a kid, I would stare at the Over-Dressed One on display with equal doses of morbid curiosity and imaginary terror. You see, I survived on a steady gluttonous diet of horror comics, movies and television shows at that age. Tales from the Crypt, The House on Haunted Hill and Dark Shadows were massive influences on my already overactive imagination.

As the adults would flock around the box, I would stand and stare at its contents. I would just stand there, my tiny hands grasping the side of the coffin, with my nose resting on the puffy, rippled material like a little morbid Kilroy. I would bide my time and, eventually, I would see it: an almost undetectable rise and fall of the chest! Young Kilroy's eyes would widen as his grip would tighten. I would mentally scream "HE'S ALIVE!" (In my head I sounded exactly like Colin Clive, by the way.) This was very plausible to me. Hell, NO ONE at Collinwood EVER stayed buried so why would Late Great Uncle Hugh?

I was convinced the cadaver in question was still alive. And, of course, I was correct in that assumption...just not in the way that I thought. There were no catatonic zombies, armies of the undead or even a colony of vampires. They were very much alive—not flesh-and-blood alive, like you and me currently—but alive in their natural state. Energy. Light. Life-force. Spirit. However you wish to categorize it is fine. I've discovered The Other Side isn't nearly as obsessed with labeling as we seem to be.

My imagination fueled me as a child and, in return, I sought out ways to stimulate it. It was an on-going vicious circle that even Mrs. Parker may have envied. I believe imagination is a key ingredient to successful mediumship. I'm not saying legitimate mediums make things up. Not by any sense of the absurd word. A vivid imagination is what allows your mind and common sense to just let go. This openness lets you welcome whatever passes by without judgment or rational thought. Of course, I had NO clue that all I was doing was adding more logs onto the roaring mediumship bonfire awaiting me. S'mores, anyone?

Time has taught me that this trail o' mine was blueprinted quite some time ago. It was being built piecemeal over a period of several years and it's STILL under construction. I was oblivious to it for the vast bulk of that time-frame. I was 40 when I realized there was a path in the first place! My construction crew, I assume, consists of Union laborers taking full advantage of their regulated breaks and work hours. Of course, as with most contractors, they never finish on time, let alone come in under budget. (I've just managed, in two short sentences, to completely alienate any union workers AND contractors who may be reading this. Note to Self: Hire a PR Manager.)

My background, my varied experiences & interests, have a bit to do with why I'm a medium. Tick that one off the list. So, what else? Someone recently said to me, "I bet there's a lot of perks doing what you do." Perks? Seriously? It's not like mediumship comes with a benefit package. I'll be honest, living a life as a medium does come at a cost. You can kiss what is perceived as normalcy goodbye. There is an alienation about this field so I hope you enjoy your own company. You have to often rely on the sound of your own voice to drown out the others echoing in your head at the most awkward of times. Predictability is predictably nonexistent. You will see things from such unusual angles that you're life will begin resembling a Dali painting. You'll even find yourself listening to someone who insists her cat is her reincarnated great grandmother who now advises her on her love life. (You have no idea how I wish I was actually making that one up…) It can be draining in all ways imaginable. And, after awhile, when you allow the voices in your head to speak over your heart—your higher self—you begin to doubt the blueprint, the contractors AND the architect.

It's at that very moment, my friends, when one can expect to be the "soul" target of an onslaught of divinely guided cream pies. Thus proving that God IS the undisputed King of Slapstick.

Tossing the realistic reasons around like a cat with a ping pong ball is not only tiring, but monotonous. This leads to dwelling on the physical, or business, aspect of mediumship. How practical is this field, really? What about doing the things I WANT to do? I do not want to rely on romantic recommendations from Tabby Grammy to fill my thoughts, let alone my schedule. So, I began looking for answers. I devoted too much of my time to turning over rocks searching for a morsel of wisdom with subzero results. What's funny about the whole thing is that my searching for the WHY had made me FORGET the why. That's like eating cheesecake as you work out on a treadmill.

Tidbits of wisdom can be found everywhere you choose to actually look AND listen. But you can look with such scrutiny that you don't see a damn thing. The whole "forest / trees" scenario, ya know? Sometimes—or, in my case—MOST of the time wisdom is hurled at me through the words of another. Why? Because figuring it out all by myself is obviously just too damn difficult. One of my favorite quotes is "For when the disciple is ready the Master is ready also." Another is, "Seek and ye shall find." And, finally, the be all and end all, "Two people kissing always look like fish."

I do not, by any means, consider myself a Master. Mediumship, like life, is just one gigantic learning curve and we're all cruising on it. I've taught some psychic & mediumship development classes over the years. Reluctantly, of course, but I've done it just the same. Teaching is not a suit I prefer to don, even though it does pop up in my wardrobe with an unsettling frequency. Like anyone else, I find myself going through the motions instead of being aware of each and every step. Instead of paying attention, I'm paying no mind to my inner and outer surroundings. I start feeling comfortable where I am in the scheme of things. Too comfortable. I end up being far too complacent in my little You-Are-Here Map. The dotted lines direct me to the rest room, any fine establishment that serves cheesecake and the Hawaiian Shirt Depot. No need to stray from what works, right? I still manage to get lost even when the dashed lines are clearly sprawled out before me. Sometimes I do it by simply standing still. Now there's a skill I need to tag onto my resume...

In the midst of my chasing my own tail from the cozy comfort of a Barcalounger, my most recent Master showed up in the form of one of my current students. Talk about adding insult to injury! He really is a very gifted medium and channel. Well, he is once he gets his own head out of the way (thank God that's NEVER the case with me... Ohhh! Lightening!). The arrow hits the bullseye and he does great... for awhile. Then he thinks and the next arrow wedges into the hillside. Eventually, he spills his quiver on the ground and stifled mayhem ensues. The battle between what the mind THINKS and what the soul KNOWS rages onward ever onward. I've told him time and time again, "You can do this!"

After relaying a rather amazing experience he had with Spirit—one that exhibited so many "coincidences" that he could open up his own museum—he wrote, "So I just wanted your opinion Charles… Is this spirit stuff real? I'm not sure if I'm fully convinced yet." At that point my head tilted to the right as my left eyebrow rose in silent sarcasm. He continued, "You NOW have the right to SMACK me during circle if I'm showing doubt or not giving the information coming to me. My guidance approves." Before I could begin oiling up my boxing gloves he allowed Spirit to work through him just a little bit more. "I feel I just have to do my homework and be available for Spirit to work through me," he realized. "It's not about ME trying to be a great medium… you may have to remind me of this from time to time…"

"So, he CAN do this," I gloated to no one in particular. Then it hit me. The little dweeb—grumbled with love—not only was handed an amazing slice of proof from Spirit for his own doubting ways, BUT they also used him to deliver a much needed sucker punch to me as well. It was even conveyed in my usual irreverent tongue-in-cheek manner. Well, goodie for them.

See? There's always reinforced construction taking place in the background. Seeking & Finding. This is much better than the usual Cease & Desist requests that I get, but I digress. It had been right there in front of me, mostly clear as day. I just refused to admit it was there all along. I caved to the voices of doubt. I gave in to the fears, and what happened? Spirit provided me with yet another array of Spiritual Wedgies and Purple Nurples.

The reason I'm a medium? The reason I allow my life to be purposely flipped upside down? The reason why I choose, every single day, to walk a path that is the equivalent of playing hopscotch in a minefield? The reason I do this work? It's simple: because I can.

Because. I. Can.

Honestly, I've never been a purveyor of normalcy. I naturally keep as many people as I can at a very comfortable distance that would overload any GPS. And routine has never been my forte. New perspectives keep an artist interested as well as interesting, don't you think? And, frankly, hearing tales of a reincarnated grand-ma-ma speaking amore through a feline is bound to make anybody's day.

I had allowed myself to shorten my naturally short-sightedness. When in doubt we tend to return to what is familiar. The same spoke, even after all these years, comes back up every now and again. Why? Is it because I haven't finished this lesson yet? Or is it because I'm digging my nails into a piece of driftwood because I'm afraid I'll drown if I let go? Fear of the unknown is a pretty funny affliction for a guy who talks to the dead.

This is where the last quote comes into play. Andy Warhol was right. Two people kissing DO tend to look like fish. But what are you actually seeing? Are you seeing a couple of mackerels making out or are you seeing a physical representation of love? Perception is the key. It can go either way but what does your natural intuition tell you? Trust what you receive. Trust what you perceive. Trust Spirit. Trust yourself. And trust the experience. I've thought, all along, that I keep repeating this serial doubt because I'm not finished with the lesson. That's the easy way out. What it boils down to is that I'm afraid to let go and trust (yet again). Well, I WAS. My anniversary gift to myself this year is making a conscious effort to let go of that driftwood and trust the waves are taking me where I need—and want—to go.

To each of you reading this, I thank you for not only trusting my connection with Spirit, but for entrusting me with the responsibility that goes with it. I am grateful for being able to do what I do. I am blessed to hopefully help you see or sense something that will bring you comfort, understanding, peace and a solid dose of healing laughter. I assure you, and myself, that I will continue to do what I do because I can for as long as I can. And, more than anything, thanks for sharing the joke with me. Laughter doesn't just lift the spirits, ya know? It lifts ALL Spirits.

So, with that in mind, two dead guys walk into a bar...

"THE SIGNS OF THE FATHER"

"Oh, I believe in coincidences. I've just never seen one."
Dannion Brinkley

I AM NOT, NOR WILL I EVER BE, A SOCIAL CREATURE. I've never been comfortable with any form of mingling. I'm more than just the brooding form huddled safely in the corner of a room. I prefer to just not show up at all. I'm that oddly placed dish of pickles on a dinner table. You don't know why it's there. Yet you pass it around to other equally disinterested guests, all the while knowing no one would miss it if it just wasn't set out in the first place. I dodge most social functions with a Gold Medal Winning Flair. I can get out of just about any social situation with nearly zero effort. It comes naturally. For example, I once had three separate invitations to Thanksgiving dinner. I got out of all of them scot-free by explaining, "Oh, how thoughtful! But I've already been invited to dinner! Thank you so much for thinking of me." Of course, I didn't attend anyone's dinner. I didn't have to go through the motions of idle banter AND I didn't have to share leftovers. Win / Win all the way around.

Even someone as expertly gifted at dodging social interaction as me gets painted into a corner from time to time. The most recent of these losses came in the form of a wedding aboard The Queen Mary last June. Of course, when I initially received the invitation, my reaction was "Oh, HELL no!" But when I realized the wedding was taking place literally within walking distance of my home I figured I was pretty much screwed. Since the best man was traveling all the way from the east coast, I couldn't really play the "It's too far for me to travel" card. Curse you, Airline Travel! Curse you and your infernal commercial conveeeeeeeenience!

Admittedly, my lack of interest in socializing was even lower than usual. My birth father, Everett, had passed away unexpectedly less than three months earlier. I was still dealing with the fallout from that, both emotionally and physically. As the executor of his estate, I had to juggle a wide array of things during that time including, but not limited to, his home & personal effects, fragile overblown egos, high-strung banshee-like emotional outbursts and why he had a plastic container filled with keys that fit absolutely NOTHING in his house. I had to push my own feelings aside (who knew I partook of such things?) and dive head-first into business mode. Which is, of course, a most clever way to not face the music (which, in my dad's case, would be performed by a trio playing a mouth harp, a set of spoons and comb kazoo).

As is my custom in social situations, I rallied a friend to join me for the festivities. The key to surviving this sort of circumstance is to find an extrovert to ever-so-slightly mask your own preferred wallflower existence. However, I could not locate such a individual. Instead, I turned to my dear friend, Mona, who may never speak to me again after reading this. Mona is not just an extrovert. Oh, no. Mona is an extrovert on crack. To the tenth power. With a dash of caffeine. Twice. She gets super excited by anything and finds everyone just gosh darn fascinating:

"Oh, my God! Tell me MORE about your masking tape collection!"

Thanks to Mona and her Perky Persona, I have met people I would have never encountered, seen things that would have stayed hidden from my farsighted baby blues, and experienced situations that would have been passed on to someone else like the aforementioned dish of pickles. I personally prefer to watch such things unfold on TV but, hey, live a little, right?

Pondering the Pavement

We donned our gay apparel and made our way to The RMS Queen Mary, permanently dry-docked here in lovely Long Beach, California. Mona was fluttering around like an ADHD kid cut loose in a candy store while I was mostly uncomfortable and bewildered. You see, I was in a situation where I had to wear long pants. LONG PANTS! And, to add insult to injury, I was informed by some misinformed fashionista that Hawaiian shirts do NOT seem to be acceptable attire with a tuxedo. I was in a foreign land where no one spoke my language.

I should mention that Mona is also a medium (we travel in gaggles, you know?). So it shouldn't come as a shock when I tell you things are bound to happen when you toss two mediums onto a haunted ship. I must admit that the vessel really is a playground for we sensitive sorts. It's where energy & ectoplasm go on vacation. Mona and I have spent a lot of time aboard the Queen Mary over the years. Mona's time on board has included taking several ghost tours, mediumship classes, and even photography field trips. In my case, however, I just get lost a lot and have a bitch of a time finding my way to an exit.

Mona was dragging me all over the ship like a six-year-old on the search for Santa at Macy's. She was excitedly pointing out different items of interest while I kept kicking myself for not leaving a trail of breadcrumbs through the corridors. Who's to say if they would have been a device to find my way out again or just a convenient snack for later in the evening...

At one point during our meandering, we encountered a tall gentleman who is the acting Commodore on the ship. He was smartly dressed in white from head to toe. (FYI: When a medium encounters someone all in white our first inclination is to poke them with a finger to ensure that they're real. That little stunt has helped me keep my Christmas card list at a VERY manageable level, let me tell ya...) Mona, as is her custom, squealed and hugged the Commodore. They exchanged pleasantries while I mentally marked all the EXIT signs within sight.

He was kind enough to chat a bit and even give us a tidbit of history of the ship—Lord knows I'm a sucker for sugar packet trivia—even though he was wrapping up his shift for the day. While he was talking I happened to glance at his name tag on his smartly pressed lapel: EVERETT. I chuckled to myself as I thought, "What a funny coincidence!"

Oh, Charles, you silly monkey. When will you learn?

The wedding was held outside on the stern of the ship. Despite no one wanting to do The Wave with me as the bride walked down the aisle, the ceremony went off without a hitch— acknowledge pun at your own discretion. All seemed right with the world as we thankfully moved inside for the reception. The groom, who is a writer among other trades, devised a deliciously unique literary theme for the reception. Each party had to search for their place card in a library Dewey Decimal card file. The names of the guests would be at the top, last name first, of course. Below the name one finds the title of a book. This tells you at what table you will be seated. Our table happened to be the Dracula Table (and it did not suck!). We made our way to our table to see the book Dracula by Bram Stoker prominently displayed as part of the centerpiece. Behind the main event was a stack of other seemingly random books. There was a Frankenstein table, a Wizard of Oz table, etc. From my point of view, the setup was nothing short of Nerdy Nirvana. Of course, the risk of possible paper cuts looming over our fingertips added a flair of exhilaration to the festivities.

The best man and his wife sat at our table. Bob and I have been close friends for nearly 40 years. That makes his wife, Shannon, my friend by default, like a step-sibling. Both of them are writers, and more, just like the groom. At one point, she sat down next to me and started talking to me like some kind of normal person. Very weird if you ask me. She said, "Remember those old photos you sent to me?"

I blanked for a moment as I searched my memory banks. All I came up with was some loose change and a green Lego. I shook my head. "Noooo…" was all I could muster.

"You sent me some old black and white snapshots," she continued, her hand delicately cradling a wine glass. "You found them and thought I'd find them interesting."

Then it dawned on me. There were several shots of some unknown small town and they were stapled together in the upper left corner. The cars captured in the images clearly eluded to the 1950's, the era of The Fonz. I had unearthed them while cleaning out one of my mother's closets. Mom had no idea why she had them or even where they were taken. Shannon is very interested in West Virginia history so I figured she'd get a kick out of them. Passing the buck for the cost of a couple postage stamps. What will I think of next?

She said, "Well, I'm using one of them in a book I'm writing so you get a photo credit."

"And I thought I'd never amount to anything!" I replied. She laughed, having no idea I was not even remotely kidding. "Do you have any idea where those pictures were taken? Or are you just using them as generic filler?"

She looked up at me as she sipped her wine. "Yea," she said. "They were taken in Everettville, West Virginia."

If I had been the one drinking I would have done a spit take that Danny Thomas himself would envy. EVERETTVILLE? SERIOUSLY?

A little while later, as Mona was running around befriending everyone on Facebook, I decided to look through the other stray books piled on our table. The ultimate wallflower looking for a book to read at a wedding reception. Jeez… how sad is THAT? I picked the first one up and opened it. I found the name of the previous owner along with a date: Carol Lundly, April 22, 1972. Everett's youngest sister goes by her middle name, Maxine, but her first name is actually Carol. And April 22nd? That just happens to be the month and day that I met my birthfather face-to-face for the very first time. I hurried and picked up the next book. The name scrawled inside of it was 'Helen', which is the first name of Everett's oldest sister.

I just sat back in my chair and began to laugh. FYI: No one thinks twice about it if you're sitting alone and laughing at a table scattered with empty wine glasses. By this time Mona had rejoined Dracula's Lair. I explained all of the connections to my dad that had popped up throughout the day. She just sat there, smugly grinning. Then I committed the ultimate sin. I asked another medium, "Do you really think it means anything?"

Mona may be tiny but she moves quickly. Her hand slapped the back of my head in a rapid cadence that gave passersby the impression they were hearing The Gettysburg Address in Morse Code. Then, in that angelic little voice of hers, she shrieked, "Do ya THINK?"

Mona's known for her sensitivity. Or so I'm told. Ahem.

Leave it to my dad, who collected wives like some people collect stamps, to make his presence known at a wedding. What else should I expect from a man who dared pass away on April Fool's Day?

If someone had come to me with this exact same story, I would be alongside Mona screaming, "DO YA THINK?" No questions asked. But when it comes to my own signs, my own connections, I end up doubting every single time. Why? I'm always leery that I'm reading too much into something. I don't want my vivid imagination to run away with me. I don't want my experiences to be simply 'wishful thinking.' That's one of the reasons my Crew tends to go over the top and slap me around. They want to make sure they have my full attention. The other reason is that they just enjoy abusing me. I think I'm their cardio workout.

The lesson? Simple: acknowledge the signs, the feelings, that you get. Even a simple "coincidence" can be your loved one's way of reaching out. Give your peeps a shout-out, a thumbs-up, for a job very well done. And know that your loved ones NEVER forget. They NEVER stop loving you. And, most importantly, they NEVER die.

Thanks, Dad, for the reminder… and so much more.

> "Laughter is the sun that drives winter from the human face."
>
> Victor Hugo

For more information on C. A. Filius and his work please check him out on the web:

www.ExtraLargeMedium.net

www.CharlesFilius.com

You can also follow him on social media:

CAFilius

@CAFilius

cfilius

Written by Charles A. Filius

(Selections From) On A Wing & A Prayer

Dailies: Day-To-Day Reminders from My Spirit Guides

Illustrated by Charles A. Filius

Clever Billy and Other Freaky, Funny Limericks*

The Flaw of Karma*

The Wayward Wand*

The Wand Goes Wild*

The Wand is Wendy*

The Secret Life of Things*

Things Alive and Other Freaky Secrets*

An Undertow of Sharks and Other New Groups*

Foster Learns A Law*

Beware of Blabbers*

Fun Net Tick Puns*

Reading is for Idjits!*

Clever Alice*

Written by W. W. Rowe

www.ingramcontent.com/pod-product-compliance
Lightning Source LLC
Chambersburg PA
CBHW061645040426
42446CB00010B/1586